The Immersive Reality Revolution

How immersive technologies will change society – for better or worse

T. P. Ffiske

ACKNOWLEDGEMENTS

I would like to thank the waterfall of coffee and tea that has fueled this book, from weekday nights to weekend days. Without them, the book wouldn't have finished.

I would also like to thank my friends and family for their support of my writing. Without them, the book wouldn't have continued.

Finally, I would like to thank Tanya Laird and Steve Dann for their Augmenting Reality meetups in London. Without them, the book wouldn't have started.

INTRODUCTION: THE IMMERSIVE REALITY REVOLUTION

For me, history is a collection of stories. Tales passed down by family members who talk about what their parents and grandparents achieved in their time alive. Or national narratives constructed by millions of people, all with a collective identity and point of origin. Some are massive and expansive, with a fantastic quality that transcends generations. Others are small but powerful, of individuals who took a step beyond the normal and forever changed the course of humanity. After a couple of years, or decades, or centuries, we collect what we know in books, videos, or films, and we sit down and say, 'this is our story, and this is how we describe ourselves.'

And what do we focus on? *Pokemon Go* and *Ready Player One.*

I get it. Both were massive and lucrative hits which used immersive technology in some way, and our community latched onto them as great examples of what the tech can do. But it's misleading. *Pokemon Go* was a massive hit because it tapped at the heart of what made the franchise popular, not because of AR (which children switched off after a period). Meanwhile, *Ready Player One* was so suffused with pop culture, like a life raft that buoyed the entire film – not because it introduced VR. In fact, it explored how we should leave the virtual world, not embrace it.

Our industry deserves better. Why don't we profile *Where Thoughts Go,* a meditative space where people can send out short confessions to each other like bubbles in the ocean? Or *Synth Riders*, a pulse-pounding dance game that builds on the mechanics laid by *Beat Saber*? Our industry is incredible, not because it rests on the successes of others, but because it stands on its own. I recognize the importance of using established IPs – we will touch on *Medal of Honor* soon – but like most, I see the astonishing original creations as well.

The stories we tell are important. They will define how we see a period in history, and we should celebrate the small and wonderful creations as well. The smallest of actions can ripple for years after, and we must track them all as much as we can.

Sometimes, historians or writers use the word 'revolution' as a turning-point in history – a point before the event, and afterwards. The aftereffects of a revolution last forever, impacting every part of human life. Technology is no exception. I firmly believe we are experiencing a new revolution that will shape every industry you can think of. We should celebrate it.

The purpose of this book is to honor the progression of augmented reality (AR), virtual reality (VR), and mixed reality (MR). All the tech strives for one goal – immersing the user in the experience. That immersion opens a new door, previously left untouched by games, writing, and films. It will continue to advance healthcare, save lives, revolutionise gaming, improve training, and so much more. We are experiencing an Immersive Reality Revolution.

But there are caveats. Any revolution can bring change, but nearly all come with casualties. The Immersive Reality Revolution will have growing pains, disrupting companies that do not use the technology properly, and facing challenges from regulators who want to temper their potential reach. The potential impact on society as well? Almost unpredictable.

But like many, I have the firm belief that it will develop and proliferate with time. Much good is happening in the industry, and it's only a matter of time before it surges forward.

There is so much potential as well. VR and AR are projected to add £62.5 billion to the UK economy, and a 2.4 per cent boost to GDP by 2030, according to a report by PwC. Globally, the figure is £1.4 trillion by the same year. The bulk of the increase will come from AR (£44.4 billion) with VR providing £18.1 billion.[1] The technology will impact 400,663 people in the future. AR will proceed to give the most significant benefits to global GDP, accounting for £985 billion of the £1.4 trillion total.

Jeremy Dalton, Head of Virtual Reality and Augmented Reality, PwC UK says: 'VR and AR are finally coming of age and have the potential to provide a significant boost to the UK economy. They will also improve the way organisations operate, make processes faster and more effective, and create incredible new experiences.

'However, the technology needs the full support of key stakeholders in order to fully prosper. Government assistance through financial incentives and funding for research and development is required, as is support for forums that handle regulatory issues as the technologies

---

[1] PwC Seeing Is Believing Report.
https://cloud.uk.info.pwc.com/seeing-is-believing-report-download. Accessed 18 Feb. 2020.

mature. Research groups will need to drive the technology forwards. And businesses will need to build a better understanding of the technology by getting started and using VR and AR to help solve business problems their organisations face.'

Then again, we are notoriously bad at predicting the future.

It became a joke in our community that people would say 'this would be the year of VR' almost every year. People predicted 2016, when the first consumer headsets entered the market. Or 2018, when the first standalone headsets were entering the market alongside stellar VR titles like *Beat Saber*. Or 2020, with the arrival of the Oculus Quest and the subsequent spike in sales.

Someone will be right. Say a thousand predictions on one topic, and one is bound to become correct. But finding substantiation for trends can be tricky or, in many cases, misleading.

Stat stories provide a significant news injection. Companies like SuperData can showcase their knowledge and predictions. Journalists, hungry for stories, taking up leads with clickable headlines. Enthusiasts share stories widely, providing the headlines to reflect their views. Research with a well-summarised headline can be shared fast and quickly across the internet – everybody wins.

Yet in many cases, research stories are wrong. SuperData announced that the Oculus Quest would become mainstream VR in 2019, but AR will lead by 2021 – a bold statement, though some doubted them as their previous statistics were wrong before. In 2016, Superdata downgraded their VR forecast, citing poor public awareness.[2]

Predictions turn false, trend timelines collapse, and distaste festers. Cynicism seeps across a community when expectations fail. Consistently, companies like SuperData have been incorrect about the immersive industry. Why might this be? Does the market have particular elements which exasperate the issue?

SuperData occupies a strong position. Owned by Nielsen, the company provides industry-leading insights into the video games market, from esports to mobile gaming. SuperData is widely trusted by its customers, which include Nintendo, Capcom and Twitch. Their role is critical – to advise customers about where to spend, and where to reinvest. Where they say, money could flow.

At times, people criticized the company for their lack of knowledge about the market, an issue many research companies face. Wrong. SuperData is incredibly invested in the market and is following its trends closely, particularly AR in mobile phones. Their network is extensive, with hundreds of developers offering thoughts on the future. A team of analysts who regularly talk to companies knows far more than a Reddit user.

SuperData is correct in one way: the immersive industry is growing. Lack of understanding is not the issue; it is the consistent overestimation of growth predictions each year.

---

[2] "SuperData: Oculus Quest Will Mainstream VR in 2019, but AR Will Lead by 2021." VentureBeat, 19 Oct. 2018, https://venturebeat.com/2018/10/19/superdata-oculus-quest-will-mainstream-vr-in-2019-but-ar-will-lead-by-2021/.

My cynical side whispers that statistics are manipulated to build better headlines. Stat categories can be expanded to include immersive companies from different areas or use revenue expectations over realistic models. The better the headline, the more publications and websites where SuperData appears.

The immersive community accepts these insights. Having well-established research companies validate their opinions is a powerful force. Yet each year, many people are growing tired of unmet expectations and now treat the stories with mild scorn.

The consensus in the immersive community is that, over time and with growing momentum, the number of companies using immersive technologies will propagate. While venture capital is down, large companies like Google and Facebook are heavily investing in technology, expecting a surge in interest over the next ten years. The industry is playing the long game. There won't be a 'year of VR'; there will be a 'decade of VR' as the technology (alongside AR and MR) slowly develops with gradual changes. Yet the timing is hard to place, which is the crux of the issue. The launch of standalone headsets led to significant jumps in revenue, though the extent is hard to predict.

The best way of using these predictions is as general industry guidance, without necessarily looking at the hard numbers. While they provide a guide on what sectors are increasing in size rapidly, their extrapolation into the future can disappoint.

Like an ageing car, the consumer ecosystem has spluttered and grown slowly. The fact prompted many companies to hold back on their VR plans for many years. Why invest so much into making a VR game or experience, when the same amount can go in other areas with higher returns?

Google would agree. The company dropped support of its Daydream platform, citing a lack of pickup. 'There hasn't been the broad consumer or developer adoption we had hoped, and we've seen decreasing usage over time of the Daydream View headset,' a spokesperson from Google told *The Verge*.[3]

Cynicism is rampant. The growth of the technology is slow, methodical, and primarily pushed by companies hoping for it to become sustainable. VR never shot up in popularity like the iPhone did over a decade ago, or the use of DVDs. It is not a fundamental part of the household.

But companies like Facebook recognize that there are several VR users who must be hit for the ecosystem to become self-sustaining. In Oculus Connect 5, Facebook said that number is ten million.[4] Once that number is hit, with the hefty backing of the company, then it becomes viable for new companies to develop and sell in the market for profit without tech giants to kick-start the system.

Then there is software. Nintendo, Microsoft and Sony handle first-party gaming titles which bring users to their platform. If a console had one of the best games of the

---

[3] Robertson, Adi. "Google Is Discontinuing the Daydream View VR Headset, and the Pixel 4 Won't Support Daydream." The Verge, 15 Oct. 2019, https://www.theverge.com/2019/10/15/20915609/google-pixel-4-no-daydream-support-view-vr-headset-discontinued.
[4] Sun, Leo. "Facebook's 3 Biggest Announcements From Oculus Connect 5." The Motley Fool, 30 Sept. 2018, https://www.fool.com/investing/2018/09/30/facebooks-3-biggest-announcements-from-oculus-conn.aspx.

last few years, then people would be willing to select a console and use it for their gaming platform of choice. The same is happening between Steam and the Epic Store, as both platforms have exclusivity partnerships with some game titles to bring gamers to them.

'Console-moving' gaming titles are vital to bringing people into VR as well. *Medal of Honor: Above and Beyond* is an Oculus Rift-exclusive title coming in 2020, using the popular IP to draw new users in. The same strategies that shaped the video games industry are now impacting the VR industry. Oculus's hires tell the same story. Jason Rubin, the VP of Special Gaming Initiatives at Facebook, co-founded Naughty Dog and ran THQ, two major gaming labels.

Above all this, one VR title stands out. Few games have left the VR gaming bubble to reach mainstream appeal. The exception is *Beat Saber*.

Beat Saber is a rhythm-based game where the player wields two laser sabers, and smashes blocks that fly towards the users to slash to the beat of the music. Think of it like *Dance Revolution* mixed with Star Wars. The aim is to hit all the blacks accurately to reach a high score.

The game enraptured the community for several reasons. The gameplay reeled players in as they sought to slash blocks of many different songs, attempting to beat their high scores. It was an addictive way to play (and for some, exercise). The game also spread quickly online, with YouTubers playing the game and showing off their skills. Some even had a green screen, placing them in the experience as they swiped to and fro. Word spread, sales skyrocketed, and *Beat Saber* reached stardom in gaming.

The title was even played by Brie Larson during the Jimmy Fallon show in early 2019. The show had millions of people watching, as they get ready for the Avengers: Endgame hype.[5] But it was also a twist-point to help VR become accepted culturally. While VR headsets are bulky and relatively unsexy, Brie Larson normalized the technology by being a celebrity having a good time with the tech, one of the most straightforward marketing techniques in modern history. As one example, Pepsi partnered with Michael Jackson to associate his stardom and style with the drink.

Acceptance is slow, but it is happening at a steady pace. It is a quiet, gradual process with a multitude of factors. Price, games, interest – all are important for the sale of hardware. Brie Larson playing in VR is another step towards acceptance, and the gameplay presented in such a way that it was entertaining, engaging, and potentially worth buying.

Beat Saber is the first VR title to hit one million sales, otherwise known as a platinum hit.[6] No small feat for a small yet vibrant community of developers and enthusiasts. It shows how software is still vital to bring new players into the ecosystem. If the purpose of VR headsets is

---

[5] "Beat Saber with Brie Larson" YouTube. https://www.youtube.com/watch?v=05pzUXujMJU. Accessed 18 Feb. 2020.
[6] Hayden, Scott. "'Beat Saber' Sells Over One Million Copies." Road to VR, 16 Mar. 2019, https://www.roadtovr.com/beat-saber-sells-one-million-copies/.

to bring gamers into the fold, then more games like *Beat Saber* need to come along.

Beat Saber is a curious example where it is platform-agnostic yet pushes the medium forward. The game can be played with multiple types of headsets and has moved hundreds of thousands of units. Many cite the game as a reason to buy a VR set. More titles like *Beat Saber* will likely come around to move more units while developing the available library for current VR users.

That said, I don't believe it should have won multiple Game of the Year awards for 2018 and 2019 respectively.

Now hold your horses. I am not saying that *Beat Saber* is a bad game; in fact, I cannot overstate how critical the success of the game has been for the adoption of VR. No wonder that Facebook acquired the company; it recognises the talent of the team and how they managed to capture an entire market.

So what tickles me is that it released in 2018. Entering Early Access that year, it built a cult following where it slowly and steadily grew an audience of passionate people who treated it as a full game – because, effectively, it was. That's twelve months of hype that backed a game released 'officially' a year later.

My views on Early Access is that, if the game is a complete product, it is the final product. The devs are confident enough with the game's quality to release it on the platform, and in turn, make money from the product. So, releasing the final build a year later feels like a misnomer, a final push to a game already in the market.

My other concern with having *Beat Saber* win Game of the Year awards in 2019 is that it shrouds the success of other games too. Take *A Fisherman's Tale*, a quiet but lovely puzzle game. It has mind-warping tasks that immerse people into the life of the sailor. While small, it has a novel and snackable quality that makes it one of the most digestible and delicious titles of 2019. And while enthusiasts in the community recognise how great the game is, it is still shadowed by *Beat Saber*.

How about *Tetris Effect*? Widely said to be one of the best versions of Tetris on the market, it is a trippy experience that oozes style, as players stack blocks and, with time, enter a daze-like state while playing the game efficiently. International champions even said that VR makes them perform better, showing how VR has a powerful effect on experienced players. But no, the game was not recognised as widely as its other blocky companion.

What about *Pistol Whip*? Similar to *Beat Saber*, it is a rhythm game which uses legs as much as the arms, with gameplay that makes people feel like a badass shooter. Or *Synth Riders*, a heart-pounding dance game that succeeds in the same way. These games build on the same genre as *Beat Saber*, with a twist. But no, the game from 2018 wins again in 2019.

I love *Beat Saber*, and the history books will remember it fondly, I just hope that the books will also not forget other titles too.

Then there is the other issue; the language we use for technological progress. While it has developed, though at a slower pace than many anticipated. Mark Zuckerberg notes that it is taking longer than expected.[7] And yes, the Oculus

---

[7] Hayden, Scott. "Facebook CEO: 'VR Is Taking Longer Than

Quest is showing signs as a game-changer in the space, with higher sales and user retention – but perhaps not enough for a juggernaut like Facebook.

But this is not a discussion on the rate of change itself; that's a topic for another time. The purpose is to pin down how we describe progress itself, and the very language we use. At best, it has been stilted, and at worst, misleading.

We use previous technology trends to compare VR, among other immersive technologies. 'VR needs its iPhone moment,' some would say. Other companies want to provide the 'Netflix of VR' with its software. While it is easy to say, and a great way to convey our thoughts, it is mostly untrue and betrays the truth of its development. VR is wholly unique, operating in its own world with its own new rules. As it has different qualities, it needs new ways to measure its qualities. As such, the development of VR must be based around 'friction', or the ease of access to VR content.

Firstly, why do we refer to previous tech trends when talking about VR? Because it is a quick and efficient way of communicating what we want. A general audience would know the story of the iPhone and how it ruptured the mobile phone market. With a smart strategy and a truly innovative design, it enraptured the world, and it soared as one of the biggest-selling products of all time. That language of progress – of having an 'iPhone moment' – has captured our language since.

Expected, But We'll See It To Mass Adoption.'" Road to VR, 4 Nov. 2019, https://www.roadtovr.com/facebook-vr-longer-than-expected-mass-adoption/.

The phrase is useful, sometimes. VR is at its early stages, where R&D is slowly catching up to user expectations. But in truth, saying we are waiting for an 'iPhone moment' is misleading. For one, we are not waiting for a brand-new contender to change the industry, when current contenders already dominate the hardware space. What's more, we are not waiting for a lower price point; iPhones in their early days were incredibly expensive. While we may be waiting for a piece of tech that makes VR comfortable, it will not be as flashy as the iPhone's touch screen. The more we unpack the phrase, the more issues we find.

On its own, VR will progress in a very different way. The barriers that face VR is different from mobile phones, revolving around accessibility and control inputs. So, we should describe VR progress in a different way. 'Friction' is the most suitable. Take the timeline of VR development over the last few years. The biggest jumps in adoption connect to the ease in which users access VR content. When the Oculus Rift launched in 2016, a small but lively group of devs adopted the headset as it was much easier to play VR games. The headset came with an online store, quality games, and at lower prices – all vital to lower the friction of entry. The same goes for the PlayStation VR, which only required users to have a PlayStation 4 in their living rooms. The headset has sold millions of headsets globally since.

Then came the Oculus Quest in 2019. With the subsequent increase in sales and adoption, there is no doubt that the Oculus Quest has upended the market. The main reason is simple – it is a standalone VR headset. No PC required, or any complicated set-up. That ease lifted the barriers of entry.

VR development shows that access is vital for adoption. The implementation of hand tracking in 2020 makes it easier for users to interact with specific software titles. Removing external sensors means people can use VR more quickly than in previous years. And when AR glasses come along, using our thoughts as inputs, then the future has truly arrived.

All this connects to the friction with the user. The less there is, the more likely someone will use VR. And the best steps for its development will likely lower it further, via lower price points, and better hardware. Neural connectivity, where our thoughts influence devices, will be the start of an entirely frictionless experience for further headsets – with its own baggage of issues we will explore later.

Regardless of how we discuss progress, what's certain is that the future is standalone. It is no surprise that Facebook is pushing the Oculus Quest hard, but is it to the extent of forsaking the Oculus Rift S, or high-fidelity VR generally?

For several years the company has made clear that they have been building towards the Oculus Quest, as the apex VR system of the generation. The purpose is to remove as much unnecessary hardware as possible, to provide an untethered and free experience. Computing power was sacrificed for portability. The focus paid off, as the company announced that the company had sold +$100m worth of software over the last few years.[8] 20 per

---

[8] "Oculus Eclipses $100 Million in VR Content Sales." TechCrunch,

cent of the sales came from the Oculus Quest alone. This is striking, as the headset was on the market for only four months at the time of the announcement.

Yet Facebook has not yet released official figures for how many Oculus Quest units they have sold, only that it's the same pace that they manufacture them.[9] The approach could be a way to mask lower than expected sales numbers. But there is no question that there has been an Oculus Quest bump for new titles, such as *SUPERHOT* selling 300 per cent more copies on the launch of the Quest than the Rift. Like the Nintendo Switch, ports are selling quickly. Financially, the Oculus Quest is making money for the company.

So, on the software side, there has been a bump in sales. But on the hardware side, Facebook is also improving the Oculus Quest's ability to use other apps.

One key example is Oculus Link, which lets users play Rift games on the platform. The product negates the need to buy a Rift S as people can buy an Oculus Quest for the same experience. Why buy an Oculus Rift S which forces the player to sit down, when they can buy the Oculus Quest and have the best of both worlds?

Then there is the cross-functionality with Oculus Go apps. Users can play certain Go apps on the Quest, meaning that they can experience the best of the previous

---

http://social.techcrunch.com/2019/09/25/oculus-eclipses-100-million-in-vr-content-sales/. Accessed 18 Feb. 2020.
[9] "Oculus Quest Devices Are Selling as Fast as Facebook Can Make Them." Android Central, 1 Aug. 2019,
https://www.androidcentral.com/oculus-quest-selling-them-fast-we-can-make-them-according-zuckerberg.

standalone headset on the new platform. Another indication that they are focusing on one platform in this case.

So, is Facebook focusing on the Oculus Quest, while the Oculus Rift S steps into the background? Not quite. Some of the most significant and impactful VR games coming over 2019 and 2020 are heading to the Oculus Rift S. *Stormland*, and *Asgard's Wrath* both went to the platform, while *Medal of Honor: Above and Beyond* will land on the same platform in 2020. The games have impressive graphics, needing the best PCs – which not everyone owns. Facebook is supporting the Oculus Rift S for the next few years, developing hardcore gaming content for the platform.

Does that mean the company will continue having three headsets in the next generation of VR? Or will the number collapse to just two, or maybe even one?

After the announcement of the Oculus Link, the next generation will likely look very different. What is more likely is that there will be a single VR headset that is both standalone, can be brought on the go, and be hooked to a PC.

Time and time again, Facebook has indicated that they want to step away from PCs eventually to have headsets that do not need the bulky machines of power. Who can blame them; not all consumers have a powerful PC. The next-generation Oculus Quest would likely be more compelling, perhaps enough to run *Stormland* and *Asgard's Wrath*. That way everybody wins, with software all coming onto one platform.

Take the Nintendo Switch. Nintendo is now focusing its home console and portable development teams into one system, focusing on one platform rather than two. New software can come more regularly, and expertise can cross-pollinate across the company. The same will likely happen as the next-generation Oculus Quest might be the only headset.

But currently, the company is not abandoning the Oculus Rift S. A lot of time, effort, and money is being invested into the platform, providing the very best experiences for players. These games would be impossible to make for the current generation of VR. But the future generation of portable VR headsets will likely be compatible with the high-end games, as their power improves. Once that happens, high-end games would be able to run anywhere outside the home.

It does not necessarily mean that developers will only focus on making portable games. Far from it. Developers would want the freedom to create compelling and expressive experiences with as much power to draw on as possible. But the ecosystem is merging.

The Immersive Reality Revolution is here. The stories we till in this time revolve around success, passion, and vigour. The blazing success of *Beat Saber*. The access of the Oculus Quest. The scrappy game devs providing new games. Companies training employees in new ways. The stories keep coming – and we will keep listening.

But be warned, readers. As the technology progresses, we will face new ethical and regulatory quandaries that shake the way we work. Like any tool, the technology can be used for evil as much as good. We will cover examples in the final few chapters.

But first, let's explore education.

EDUCATION: TEACHING FUTURE GENERATIONS WITH IMMERSIVE TECH

What are your favourite ways of learning a topic? For some, it is reading a textbook and using flashcards to imprint the knowledge onto the mind. For others, it is watching YouTube videos. Each person has particular ways of learning about something new, and many innovative developers are keen to hop onto the new way to teach.

Immersive technologies have their perks. For one, students are less likely to be distracted by their phones if they have a headset strapped to their face. More importantly, there is a wealth of evidence that immersive teaching is effective.

Barbara DeHart, Co-Founder of Sama Learning, wanted to find out how. Ms DeHart experimented with over 1000 students across three universities to see if learning STEM in a virtual reality device improves the education process.[10] Ms DeHart designed the experiment to evaluate deploying VR at scale, and their positive impact in classrooms.

Ms DeHart and her team discovered that virtual reality in classrooms had a positive effect. Taking into account before and after testing, and control trials, the team found that students improved by a full letter grade. It showed that immersive tech leads to an improvement in learning. The team also found that students had an appetite for further experiences, showing that virtual reality has a

---

[10] Ffiske, Tom. "Virtual Reality in Education: What Is the Future?" Virtual Perceptions, 22 Aug. 2019,
https://www.virtualperceptions.com/virtual-reality-education-future/.

pull beyond initial testing. It is not to say that the technology should replace whiteboards. People should use tools to help teach students, and not one device should dominate. But the experiment shows that there is a clear link between VR and improved memory retention.

As another example, Two CITS Affiliates, Professors Dorothy Chun and Richard Mayer, are researching the effects of immersive technologies in the classroom, and how they are useful as additional tools of education.[11] The team addressed the topic via multiple approaches as they combined computer scientists with education researchers.

The authors hypothesized that AR could greatly help with learning foreign languages via an overlay of labels on objects. Imagine walking around home and seeing an array of objects labelled in another language, immersing yourself in the language each day. When making tea, cleaning the house, or travelling to work, users absorb new words.

The study used the Microsoft HoloLens, and participants were in a room observing the objects and their corresponding labels. Afterwards, participants tested their knowledge by being shown images of said objects and reciting their foreign language term, both immediately after the event and several days after. The researchers compared the results to a sub-group who learned a foreign language through more traditional means, the flashcard-based method.

---

[11] Bringing Augmented and Virtual Reality to the Classroom | Center for Information Technology and Society - UC Santa Barbara. https://cits.ucsb.edu/news/announcement/650. Accessed 18 Feb. 2020.

Remarkably, the AR group performed better by 7 per cent than the same-day testers. The difference widened when the test was taken several days after, with a 21 per cent difference.

There are many reasons why this may be. I suspect one might be the use of new technologies excited the participants, meaning the learning experience was more impactful for the user when compared to simple flashcards. Another reason may be usability. When walking around a familiar home, words associated with everyday objects leads to a positive association when learning a new language. It is one thing to learn the name of a TV; it is another to look at your TV and see the Spanish translation of something you own.

Students could explore virtual versions of locations they cannot access otherwise. So, one of the best ways of using the technology is field trips.

For those restricted to their local area for financial or mobility reasons, it's a great way to see new places. Why fly to Italy, when people can visit Italy in their rooms? National Geographic VR lets users climb mountains or explore ocean depths, well beyond the budget of most schools.[12] Learning about another country or their culture feels more real if people can visit locations in person. While it pales to the real world, it offers a glimpse which surpasses books and their text.

---

[12] Society, National Geographic. "Virtual Reality at Nat Geo." National Geographic Society,
http://www.nationalgeographic.org/events/event/virtual-reality/.
Accessed 18 Feb. 2020.

Virtual reality field trips can transcend not only distance but time as well. Students can visit Ancient Greece, interacting with the great philosophers of the time. Or visit Thailand's ancient capital a long time ago. Experiences such as *MasterWorks: Journey Through History* gives users a history lesson without needing a DeLorean.[13]

Such experiences complement their education. Imagine learning Latin, which comprises of learning conjunctions and words of a language long dead. A virtual reality trip to Ancient Rome can enliven the learning experience, granting content to their education.

Chris Lewis, an IT lecturer and Head of HND Computing from Grantham College, ran experiments to find out more. The first experiment is linking all his students in *AltspaceVR* and gave personalised feedback to his students within the virtual world. The volume of the interactions was related to the students' proximity to each other, so they directly heard their feedback. Meanwhile, those further away were not distracted from their work. This personalised kind of interaction is more tailored to individual students. So far, so exciting.

Then Mr Lewis used A-Frame, a WebVR experience creator, to produce tableaux which students can interact with, then imported it into *AltspaceVR*. He let the students interact with the animations and wander around the item. Mr Lewis found that they engaged with the content and enjoyed using it.

---

[13] "Masterworks: Journey Through History Provides A Transformative Educational VR Experience." VIVE Blog, 1 Oct. 2018, https://blog.vive.com/us/2018/10/01/masterworks_vr_experience/.

There are many examples like this across multiple classrooms. All found that it is not enough to have a virtual class to teach lessons. For teachers to make the most of virtual reality in education, human interaction is a must.

Up to this point, researchers explored virtual reality in great detail. By placing students in VR, they can learn new things to complement their education. But what about augmented reality, the tech found on phones that can put an overlay on a real-life object?

If used correctly, it absolutely can. Curiscope creates shirts that have body parts on them, which children can wear. Then, the students can use their app to see through the shirts, showing the working human body under the skin. It is a neat way of showing how the human body pumps blood across the human body, as a supplementary way of learning biology.

Augmented reality is an excellent way of teaching children, provided the content is right. As most people have a smartphone, it is a unique out-of-pocket way of trying new things. However, it requires the concerted effort of the students to download apps and hold their attention long enough to interact with new apps. But once this barrier is lept, a new world can unveil itself for the teacher and the classroom.

So which headset to pick? The best VR headsets depend on the budget which schools have, and the quality that students may like to experience:

- **Google Cardboard**. The most accessible way to experience immersive content. The cardboard viewer lets people slot in their smartphone and watch content via YouTube. It is also great to use with kids. In practice, it is not VR; it is a 360 video which people cannot interact with. There are some great videos on the platform, but it pales to the true VR which the other headsets provide.

- **Oculus Go.** A standalone VR headset for those who want to dip their toes into VR. Users control the virtual environment via a 3DoF controller, which means it operates on a virtual pivot with less control than its high-end counterparts. But it still features some great experiences, such as *National Geographic VR, VR Vienna*, and *World Traveler VR*. As it does not need a computer to run, it is easy to transport around the classroom.
- **Oculus Quest**. A step up from the Oculus Go, the standalone VR headset offers 6DoF controls and room-scale VR, which means players can walk around a room and interact with their surroundings. Some great experiences include *Wander* and *Apollo 11*.
- **Oculus Rift S**. Much like the HTC Vive line, this is the most high-end experience, giving students the very best quality for gameplay. However, it is also the most expensive, and it is reliant on having a PC for use. What's more, the Oculus Go and Oculus Quest both provide great experiences without the price tag. Because of this, I recommend other headsets.

But most importantly, it depends on the scale of the experience. If it is small and low fidelity, pick a smaller headset. If it is vast and expansive, go big.

If convinced, the next step is to pick a VR headset; but which one? From taking field trips to teaching a virtual classroom, VR technology has potential for helping students. Here are some tips for the aspiring teacher:

- **Clean the VR headset after use.** If there is only one headset shared by multiple students, then it will collect sweat and grime with time. The experience can lead to a greasy, unpleasant peripheral by the end of the day. Wipe down the headset whenever it changes heads, ideally with a tissue and an alcohol-based washing liquid. When dry, place on the next individual.
- **Pick the right experiences.** With the amount of software available, it can be challenging to choose the right one to complement teaching. Think more widely and consider what's best for the classroom. Is it a virtual class? *AltspaceVR* provides the capabilities for education. Is it to complement learning a language, like French? Pick one that lets people travel to France. Get creative!
- **Check the software for warning labels.** Virtual reality in education can be overwhelming, and some students may not feel comfortable with it. Some games may also have photosensitivity warnings, depending on what they contain. Check the software before letting the students have a go.

In summary, the uses of virtual reality in education are extensive. With the flow of financing uplifting new projects, children will experience new ways of learning content. While slow, progress is steadily moving forward. Yet it depends on which areas, and how far.

Robin de Lange, Director at the Virtual Reality Learning Lab, has a realistic vision of the future: 'VR is earning its place as a powerful learning tool. Research shows that the suspicions we had might be right. But that's not to say that VR is the best decision for every type of learning material and every type of classroom situation.

'VR will not disrupt the school or the classroom anytime soon. However, it will be used more and more in situations that really benefit from it.'

Robin's nuanced approach summarises the role of virtual reality in the classroom: as a tool to support students alongside other devices. Instead of dominating teaching as the sole approach, People can use the tech to guide learning with different ways of engaging students. Even augmented reality has its place as well, for similar reasons. Like using whiteboards to illustrate points, or videos to visualise concepts, virtual reality offers another way to engage and discover new content. Virtual reality and education can work hand-in-hand.

The same applies to AR. For VR, the technology grants motivation, but not as good for learning unless creators shape the experience for it. Professor Richard Mayer and Jocelyn Parong then used VR to learn about biology and did two experiments. In the first, one group watched a lesson in biology via *The Body VR: Journey Inside a Cell,* while the other viewed a basic PowerPoint slide on the same topic. Those learning from a slide scored an average of 3.5 points higher (out of 20) than those who learned in VR. Participants noted that they enjoyed the experience and engagement, though it did not transition to a higher score afterwards.

The team experimented again, with two groups. The first watched the experience as usual. The second had the same experience broken into chunks and pauses, where students summarized what they learned. On average, this group scored 3.5 points higher than the former group.[14]

The research team surmised that 'VR is an effective tool to prime student's interest and motivation toward a given subject,' and that a generative learning strategy worked with VR. It seems VR provides inspiration yet needs to be applied appropriately to maximize impact.

Like with any tool, the way it's applied is everything. AR can help with learning foreign languages. VR motivates a subject, yet not have an impact unless the creator made the experience for learning. Cutting-edge technologies are shiny and new, with each wave bringing in new innovators to hop onto the surfing trend.

Yet though the benefits are likely excellent, there is a time and a place for their application. Sometimes, there are much more efficient ways of investing in education which is much more cost-effective and useful for students. Currently, the UK is having issues with the education system, as classes grow in size and overworked teachers

---

[14] Parong, Jocelyn & Mayer, Richard. (2018). Learning Science in Immersive Virtual Reality. Journal of Educational Psychology. 10.1037/edu0000241.

churn out of the system within a few years.[15] Schools need essential equipment, not necessarily VR headsets.

Some companies are generously donating into the system to help. Oculus gave headsets to schools for education.[16] Yet at a time where basic items are not available, it is superfluous to ask schools to use VR in their education system.

In any case, researchers proved the link between immersive tech and learning. For the small percentage who can access them, it can help with education. But for the rest? I would focus on other areas first.

---

[15] Weale, Sally, and Richard Adams. "'It's Dangerous': Full Chaos of Funding Cuts in England's Schools Revealed." The Guardian, 8 Mar. 2019. www.theguardian.com,
https://www.theguardian.com/education/2019/mar/08/its-dangerous-full-chaos-of-funding-cuts-in-englands-schools-revealed.

[16] Statt, Nick. "Oculus Is Bringing Its Rift and Go VR Headsets to Classrooms around the World." The Verge, 28 Aug. 2018,
https://www.theverge.com/2018/8/28/17792166/oculus-vr-rift-go-headsets-education-classrooms-taiwan-japan-seattle.

EMPATHY: THE POWER OF IMMERSION TO CHANGE LIVES

Gunfire blazed across the sky, their fluorescent light igniting the night. People wailed and cried, running away or crawling into the fetal position, shivering. Children cower with them, clutching their arms tightly. Bodies litter the floor like piles of rags.

The news channel moves to the next story.

News articles explore issues around the world in detail, complementing quotes from authoritative figures with insightful statistics. Reports provide an overview, a snippet of experience based on the first-person perspective of the reporter. Yet with time, these articles become numb. A tsunami hits a city and kills 1,222 people; a number which may seem small, but only in the context of other disasters that report thousands more. The death of 1,222 people impacts thousands of family members, some reliant on their work and income. The number fills a school hall.

Yes, publications inform the population. But in reality, they provide such a deluge of informative news on disaster after disaster, both small and large, that the human mind numbs it all. A school shooting becomes normal, a side-story alongside domestic politics. Twitter posts of cute cats scroll alongside an update on a bloody conflict somewhere else in the world. We become passive observers. We lose empathy.

So, what can reporters do to bring more life and impact to a story? Pictures work to illustrate a conflict, but there are only so many times it works. Videos take the next logical step, providing footage of what's happened. The description of guns pales to their actual use. Seeing soldiers fighting, nearly getting shot, engages viewers much more than the story of their fight. Visual storytelling changes culture.

Here is where VR comes in. Why read about a conflict, or watch a battle, when you can observe within it? Or, even better, why not build empathy in other areas in culture – perhaps along racial and cultural lines?

Owen Cotterall from Juice Immersive agrees: 'At a very human level, this unlocks massive potential for increased awareness and understanding of the lives of other people and beings far removed from our own. Consequently, this new level of insight can drive huge uplifts in empathy for those whose shoes, for the first time, we now have the ability and privilege to 'walk in'. For me, there is no better demonstration of the power of immersive reality to change outlooks, to change lives, and to make the world a better place.'

Companies tackle racial bias in numerous training programmes; a notable example is Starbucks in 2018, who shut 8,000 of its stores for training.[17] Organisers delicately handle the situations to educate their employees in the best way possible. These pieces of training are essential. Yet if the training was mishandled, it could lead to unfortunate consequences. In some cases, employees walk away from sessions feeling shame or shaken by the experiences. These

---

[17] Hyken, Shep. "Starbucks Closes 8,000 Stores For Racial Bias Training -- Is It Enough?" Forbes,
https://www.forbes.com/sites/shephyken/2018/06/01/starbucks-closes-8000-stores-for-racial-bias-training-is-it-enough/. Accessed 18 Feb. 2020.

experiences hurt the mental health of employees who work in the company.

Clorama Dorvilas designed a VR experience to remove the shame and guilt felt afterwards, via debiasing techniques. 'Companies can spend millions of dollars on extremely ineffective, and virtually useless training that can have an adverse effect which can hurt the company even more,' she said. 'Bias training shouldn't be there to shame. People should feel good about making others feel accepted. Debias isn't something that you can work out in a day. It's a behaviour that you have to work through. We want to give people the capacity to work in a safe and comfortable space.'[18]

Dorvilas found that empathy allowed people to humanize each other and applied that to VR. Numerous studies show that unconscious bias impacts education and teaching, as it shapes how people teach and how they see relative achievement. The approach shaped the creation of Teacher's Lens, an app which provides simulations in VR and reduces bias safely and comfortably. The app presents the teacher with a racially diverse classroom and tracks how they act.

Let's move on to a different kind of empathy. For the longest time, I never cared to switch to alternative kinds of milk. Veganism was an alternative movement where people forsake eating meat, for depressing salads and carrot sticks.

---

[18] Young, Tyler. "This VR Founder Wants to Gamify Empathy to Reduce Racial Bias." Vice, 20 July 2018, https://www.vice.com/en_us/article/a3qeyk/this-vr-founder-wants-to-gamify-empathy-to-reduce-racial-bias.

I couldn't connect with veganism, because I couldn't quite put myself in their shoes. I read plenty about the health benefits, how it helps the planet, and how it is more efficient to grow crops than feed animals; but nothing touched me enough to switch from milk to something else. It was just a massive blank to me.

I've known full well about the exploitative food industry, about how cows are used and abused. I knew, but I never fully understood it. It was always a nebulous concept, a far-away idea that cows lived in abnormal conditions, but it never quite visualized in my brain. All of this happened after a torrent of articles, documentaries, and books — a deluge of facts, passing out of my mind.

Then I saw iAnimal, an immersive experience from Animal Equality. The five-minute 360 video charts the life of a cow over five minutes, from being pulled out of the mother's womb at birth to being slaughtered for its meat. Narrated by Evanna Lynch, the experience charts the cow's life and how the dairy industry exploited it for milk, alongside the conditions it endured.

After watching the experience, I promptly switched from drinking milk to alternatives made by soya or oat. I should stress I am still a meat-eater. Some habits are hard to break. But the experience deeply challenged my views on veganism and changed my habits in a small way.

Why is this significant? For me, this marked the first time that immersive technologies shaped my behaviour, more than articles, videos, or even documentaries. None of these changed my habits, but one five-minute immersive experience changed the way I drink from then onwards. The video was one proof case where

34

immersive technologies can have a significant impact on someone's life.

VR provides an empathy tool for other projects, such as films. One recent example is *Virtually History: The Berlin Wall.* Created in collaboration with Remarkable and YouTube Originals, the team designed the short pieces as though users can step into a photograph of the past.[19] While simple, the videos offer a compelling and engaging way to learn about the Berlin Wall, which we recommend anyone to watch.

The creatives gave a preamble before the viewing, outlining their intentions of creating an educational way of learning about East and West Germany. All of the experiences show different and impactful perspectives of the people living through the event. One shows a family running away before the wall fell. Another group was digging a tunnel under the deathstrip. All showed a fierce, repressed struggle marked those on both sides, as loved ones split and remained apart.

The images were fascinating – we got to experience compelling situations such as a family fleeing from their home through their window, and an image taken the day the wall fell.

The most remarkable photograph brought to life for this project is probably one of a man digging a tunnel. Klaus Keussler, a student in West Germany at the time, and his friends worked for months to build a tunnel to East

---

[19] Ffiske, Tom, and Mandahus, Lena. "Virtually History: The Berlin Wall." Virtual Perceptions, 6 Nov. 2019,
https://www.virtualperceptions.com/virtually-history-the-berlin-wall/.

Germany, to create an escape route. The tunnel became known as Tunnel 57 (named after the number of people who escaped through it).

Building such a tunnel was highly dangerous, as it was prone to flooding, could collapse at any time, and of course, highly forbidden. The experience not only makes the photo of Klaus digging the tunnel come to life, but it also transports the viewer into the bottom of the shaft. Hearing that a tube is just wide enough for one person to slither through on hands and knees is one thing, but getting to 'stand' in it in VR brings the matter closer to an audience than any history or regular documentary can.

A narrator tells the story around the image and gives historical context, while users observe various colourised images of the event. Experiencing history by stepping into a picture is an experience that makes a long-lasting impression, mainly when it covers a tumultuous and complicated time in history, such as the Iron Curtain.

The critical question is, why 360 video? What does the experience give that books and films cannot? While simple, the illusion of immersion is convincing. Though the images do not move, the small and subtle sounds used – the shovel of dirt, the clatter of running shoes – makes the still photographs feel alive.

The experience is undoubtedly a step up from reading a book; no book can recreate the cries of a mother's grief. But a documentary provides a compelling way to learn about the Berlin Wall, where archive footage and testimonials make a recent historical event feel vibrant. If comparing between the two, *Virtually History: The Berlin*

Wall matches that of any excellent documentary on the same subject.

But perhaps that's not the best way to think of it, as a directly comparable piece. Instead, maybe it should be a supplement, an addition to an education on the Berlin Wall. Textbooks can give an overview, and documentaries can go into greater detail, but even an excellent documentary cannot quite capture being inside Tunnel 57. That inclusiveness, though simple, is an effective storytelling technique.

Virtually History: The Berlin Wall offers several short and engaging pieces on a fascinating period in history. Snippets into people's lives provide colour to a grey period, as people bring the stories to life.

Though simple, the films are compelling. For creatives working in the industry, it shows how simple approaches can have powerful effects on viewers, and while building empathy as well.

SOCIAL SPACES: SHAPING THE WAY WE COMMUNICATE WITH ONE ANOTHER

Can VR replace pubs, cafes, and other social areas? Can people have deep and meaningful conversations without being in the same place, interacting via virtual avatars?

To many, the concept seems ludicrous. Two people sitting in their rooms donned with VR headsets and thousands of miles apart, feels a little off. What interactions can match seeing someone you care about face-to-face? And when split by distance, what matches the ease of using video chat and sitting comfortably? It could be an unnecessary step when we can easily interact in other ways.

Rupert Breheny, VR Manager at Google, found that the isolated nature of VR could be social depending on the application: 'So many VR experiences can be isolating. You are removed from the people around you and it is not an inherently social experience. But we've found that when people use Google Earth, they then start to tell stories to each other.'[20]

But there are compelling and persuasive reasons for why VR social spaces could pick up over time. Research has shown that different setups can influence how we interact, and it can be more potent than a simple video call.

Our social situations impact how we talk to one another. Pubs bring a colloquial sense of banterous discussion, while events requiring a suit brings a more

---

[20] "Rupert Breheny (Google): Enabling Immersive Exploration with Google Earth VR" YouTube.
https://www.youtube.com/watch?v=sjqR90XGRDs. Accessed 24 Feb. 2020.

measured demeanour. These same influences impact virtual spaces as well. Hubs by Mozilla tested users in different areas, while Mozilla partnered with Jessica Outlaw and Tyesha Snow of The Extended Mind to review the user experience of the platform.[21]

The team found that smaller spaces promoted conversations. In larger areas, when the team enabled exclusive audio, participants felt they didn't connect to others as they moved away from them. The consequence occurred because the further away they were, the lower the speaker volume, meaning the more isolated the user became. The Extended Mind team concluded that the type of space influenced behaviour; a more extensive area pulled users to explore, while a smaller office-like space promoted intimate discussions. In a sense, size matters (in design). The contents of the room changed how users saw its purpose as well. Adding a door which cannot be opened meant one user saw the space as an interrogation room: a fabrication in their mind rather than the intention of the designers.

The team concluded that creators should consider the environment's design and how users may interpret them. I agree with this. Video game designers say that the first level is one of the most important, as it introduces the main mechanics of the game and slowly unfolds them in an accessible way. Nintendo designed the first level of Super Mario Bros. on the NES so that someone who has never played a video game before can learn the rules of the game.

---

[21] "How XR Environments Shape User Behavior." The Extended Mind, https://extendedmind.io/blog/2018/11/13/how-xr-environments-shape-user-behavior. Accessed 18 Feb. 2020.

It first places players in a safe space where they can mash buttons to work the controls, then guides them through the first set of obstacles to introduce new elements such as enemies and items.

The idea bleeds to social space design as well. If the world is vast and sprawling, littered with items to interact with, the user will explore. If it is a small bar, then people will more likely play with drinks and have conversations. If it is a party room, people will dance. Design defines actions.

All of this leads to the overarching question of how we interact in the future. Earlier in the book, we explored how friction should be the language of progress. The same concept applies here as well – the easier it is for people to interact, the more likely that it'll develop. Calling became popular as a quick way to talk to friends. Then texting arrived, as a fast method to send and log messages. And video calls put a face to their words.

Would avatars talking in a room come next? Perhaps. If loved ones are far away, talking to a virtual version may be better than, say, texting. At the same time, it seems superfluous. Why not just video chat? Why not see the real face, not a created façade?

A company that stands to benefit from the approach is, you guessed it, Facebook. Currently, friends communicate privately over Messenger – but in that way, they cannot connect to new people. Groups are one way to have discussions, but it's distant, like sending letters out to cyberspace. So I can see Facebook Horizons, their new project, focusing around people with shared interests entering a room to discuss their opinions, out loud, with others in a virtual area. The approach creates a community, one where people can express themselves more while meeting new people.

Of course, the approach would be riddled with issues. Every area cannot be a safe space, and persuasive people can coerce others to poor actions. Or worse. But all the same, Facebook is designing the metaverse to facilitate conversations.

So I can see avatars used among groups. Perhaps not with friends or family, but certainly to connect with new people and make new friends. Similar things happened with World of Warcraft. We will see if people care enough to adopt the approach and step in.

AR GLASSES: THE NEXT BIG TECH BATTLE

At the moment, we have Oculus, HTC, Microsoft, and many other headset developers vying for control of the VR market. Oculus is making significant headway with their Oculus Quest, while HTC is doubling down on the enterprise level with the HTC Vive Pro.

Yet in the background alongside VR, AR glasses are steadily getting better and improving their capabilities, quietly and surely. Facebook, Apple, Huawei, and others are developing their versions.

AR glasses already populate the market. Vuzix is a leading developer with cutting-edge technology and patents, while the Google Glass spluttered some lift into the ecosystem (before coming back again). Yet a new wave will come soon, as rumours of Apple and Facebook are developing their consumer-end versions whisper across the internet. Magic Leap lept into AR in 2018, with a new version in production, then went quiet for a short period; we should expect more activity from them through 2020.

Meanwhile, WaveOptics is making waveguides and projectors for AR wearables. The company is interesting because they lay out the foundational components for the immersive revolution. From the smart Katana-class to the wide Odin, they supply the necessary parts for other companies. They also point out that we should see some activity from late 2020 onwards.

WaveOptics invited Virtual Perceptions to their Oxford-based offices, to try out the latest waveguides and projectors they are developing for their NDA-locked clients. The day started with their principal announcement, the Katana, alongside showing us their lab.

Waveguides and projectors are the components that project a screen on a lens, which in turn augment the world with an overlay. Their demos ranged from small notifications that appear at the edge of a screen, to watching football matches over a massive screen. While some companies like Vuzix create all parts of AR glasses, WaveOptics focuses on supplying critical AR components to interested clients who want to mass-produce their own.

I came because I wanted to see the technology behind the glasses of the future. What are the components that enable AR glasses to work the way they do? And how far has the technology progressed over the last few years?

It turns out, very far.

The purpose of inviting Virtual Perceptions was to introduce the Katana under embargo. The waveguide is designed for consumer-level AR glasses, weighing just 7g. It aims to combat the main barriers of AR adoption: cost, design, and power usage. The company claimed that, by designing for all three factors, it has the right lens for some of their clients.

The company sees it as a pivot-point: 'Katana is pushing the boundaries of what's possible for augmented reality headsets, bringing mass-market ambitions closer to reality,' said David Hayes, CEO of WaveOptics.

'As the thinnest, full-colour waveguide available on the market, Katana enables our customers to design new products that can meet the performance expectations of a wider range of consumers, and we can help them do that at the right price point. As 5G takes off and the focus turns to wearables, we are looking forward to seeing what our customers will do with this technology.'

WaveOptics demoed the Katana in an adjacent room. I was impressed by the lightness and how crisp the image was as well. It showed a model of a car engine spinning around, with details of each part around it.

What struck me also was how wide the FOV was as well. I've always been used to small, constrictive squares which show little of the AR, breaking the immersion. The Katana bucked my preconception by filling my eyes with the content, far further than I expected. (The Odin-class waveguide was even more significant and very impressive).

WaveOptics is also interesting because they are knee-deep in the future of AR. Their CEO also suggested that, on the enterprise level, they can be used to create second screens while working on a computer.

The demo showed that technology has gone a long way compared to their competition and that new customers will be surprised by how crisp and clear the image is alongside how big the FOV has become. I can also see why they specialised so deeply; when they took us around the lab, my brain fried a little with the explanation for how the tech worked. The way projected light is bent to make an image is both astonishing and, in part, beyond my comprehension. But it works, and it works wonderfully.

WaveOptics will not yet disclose whom they are working with. But with Panasonic and Samsung entering the market, it would be interesting to see how the competition heats up. And, as with any market, it's always important to keep track of the suppliers of components.

Yet their societal impact will be seismic, rupturing the way people communicate and work. Mobile phones changed social conventions and the way we socially communicate. AR glasses will do the same.

Short-sightedness is on the rise across the world. In Seoul, over 95 per cent of men aged 19 have myopia, the clinical word for the standard condition. Some estimates say that one-third of the world's population could be affected by it by the end of this decade. A lot of people will need a new pair of specs.[22]

The reasons for the sharp rise vary from education to electronics, yet the point remains the same – we all need glasses. The glasses industry is currently worth over £100bn.[23] Glasses are not a fun toy to buy, like a games console or a set of headphones. The specs act like a utility, a necessary part of someone's life. Dominate a market, and you act like a utility company who provides the absolute necessities of family life. The tech giants spotted the trend and want to dominate the market.

Vuzix is a current leading player in the market, serving powerful sets which brings a punch, for a price. The company has a high share-of-voice in the sector, coming up as the first results for AR glasses. Like vines, they cling to the phrase with a tight grip, melding themselves to the trend as much as possible.

Over time, the strategy worked. Vuzix recently announced that its Blade Smart Glasses can now be sold in

---

[22] Dolgin, Elie. "The Myopia Boom." Nature News, vol. 519, no. 7543, Mar. 2015, p. 276. www.nature.com, doi:10.1038/519276a.
[23] "Global Eyewear Market Value 2018-2025." Statista, https://www.statista.com/statistics/300087/global-eyewear-market-value/. Accessed 18 Feb. 2020.

Japan, meaning it now sells across 35 countries.[24] The company hopes consumers use the glasses instead of their phones. Paul Travers, President and CEO of Vuzix, is hopeful for the future. As he says, 'Vuzix Blade Smart Glasses can deliver content alerts and information to consumers without taking their phones out of their pockets.'

Paul notes that the company has a significant amount of interest. 'Some of the largest wireless carriers in the world across North America, Europe, and Asia, have shown strong interest in deploying our waveguide and smart glass technologies products for their wireless networks soon and see its ability to drive cellular services, including 5G, and provide a competitive advantage.'

Its expansion and popularity on shows such as CES indicate a healthy and robust company. The insight is in contrast with the bulky Google Glass, which crept into the background after some lousy marketing, a hefty price tag, and lack of adoption.

Yet Apple will arrive to stand alongside Magic Leap. And Facebook is not far behind. When these tech behemoths come into the market, that's when we expect competition to heat up.

In October 2018, Facebook confirmed they are making their own AR glasses.[25] Ficus Kirkpatrick, Head of

---

[24] Vuzix Expands Market Access for Vuzix Blade Smart Glasses to 35 Countries with the Addition of Japan□:: Vuzix Corporation (VUZI). https://ir.vuzix.com/press-releases/detail/1676/vuzix-expands-market-access-for-vuzix-blade-smart-glasses. Accessed 18 Feb. 2020.

[25] "Facebook Confirms It's Building Augmented Reality Glasses." TechCrunch, http://social.techcrunch.com/2018/10/24/facebook-ar-headset/. Accessed 18 Feb. 2020.

Augmented Reality at the company, told TechCrunch that 'we have a lot of very talented people doing compelling cutting-edge research that we hope plays a part in the future of headsets.'

It's clear that this is the next logical leap for Facebook. Currently, they are reliant on the mobile headsets of Apple, Google, and other handset manufacturers. Taking control of the hardware itself, like Apple, brings more power. Smartphones dominate the crowded market, where the growth markets are in the emerging regions. The time is right to diversify.

Will Facebook's AR efforts conflict with its VR division? Not at all. Oculus' Chief Scientist Michael Abrash said that VR offers rich, immersive experiences for the home, as a new platform for play.[26] Glasses are a socially acceptable equivalent which is more socially acceptable than a bulky headset.

Facebook harvests users' data, not without criticism. To extend their capacity to collect data, they need to track users when they are not checking their phone. Instead of tracking habits when they're in the bathroom, they collect data when they are socializing, having fun, or seeing family.

Meanwhile, across the industry, there are whispers that Apple AR glasses are on their way. Sleek and stylish, the specs are the next natural step for Apple and its brand. Very little is known about them at this time. Except for

---

[26] Robertson, Adi. "Oculus Is Trying to Make the Quest the Only Home Headset That Matters." The Verge, 27 Sept. 2019, https://www.theverge.com/2019/9/27/20885082/oculus-quest-home-headset-lineup-oc6.

pieces of information either leaked from Apple, or are extrapolated from their corporate filings and acquisitions.

For example, in 2014, Apple acquired Luxvue, a company creating tiny, super-bright displays; useful if fixed to the lens of glasses.[27] Other companies followed: Sensomotoric, which does eye tracking;[28] Vrvana, an AR headset;[29] and Metaio together with Flyby, both AR startups.[30] These movements raise several flags that Apple has been developing AR applications for many years.

Patents complement the acquisitions. In 2018, the US Patent & Trademark Office published a patent application that describes devices that place AR Maps on a surface.[31] We should treat patents with care – they are made to protect assets, and not necessarily indicate an ongoing development project. But it's fair to track for now, in case further hints appear down the line.

---

[27] "Apple Acquires Power Efficient LED Tech Company LuxVue." TechCrunch, http://social.techcrunch.com/2014/05/02/apple-acquires-power-efficient-led-tech-company-luxvue/. Accessed 18 Feb. 2020.
[28] "Apple Acquires SMI Eye-Tracking Company." TechCrunch, http://social.techcrunch.com/2017/06/26/apple-acquires-smi-eye-tracking-company/. Accessed 18 Feb. 2020.
[29] "Apple Acquired Augmented Reality Headset Startup Vrvana for $30M." TechCrunch, http://social.techcrunch.com/2017/11/21/apple-acquires-mixed-reality-headset-startup-vrvana-for-30m/. Accessed 18 Feb. 2020.
[30] "Apple Acquires Augmented Reality Company Metaio." TechCrunch, http://social.techcrunch.com/2015/05/28/apple-metaio/. Accessed 18 Feb. 2020.
[31] "Apple Patent Describes Tangibility Visualization of Virtual Objects within Various Headset Environments." Patently Apple, https://www.patentlyapple.com/patently-apple/2019/11/apple-patent-describes-tangibility-visualization-of-virtual-objects-within-various-headset-environments.html. Accessed 18 Feb. 2020.

Apple's move to AR makes sense. The company is taking several steps to make their technology not only functional, but also stylish. The iWatch displays its capabilities in a variety of fashionable icons, dominating the watch market afterwards. Apple understands that its products are a desirable fashion statement; its products designed so that users can be proud to show them off.

So what about Magic Leap? The Magic Leap One: Creator Edition launched in August 2018. After the unicorn hid under a mountain for several years, it finally jumped out – to find it was not as magical as people expected. Games like Angry Birds showed the potential of the device, yet it is not the graphical powerhouse which initial trailers revealed over the last few years. While the concept is there, the hardware needs more work.

That said, Magic Leap started several creator programs to finance people to make applications for the product. Recognizing the need for great software, the company is building goodwill with the developer community by helping and guiding projects. Magic Leap is building the foundation for a robust second go.

So we have several technology companies potentially vying to become the AR spectacles of the future. Assuming decent price ranges, low regulation, and consumer trust, AR glasses will get some modest pickup through the 2020s. What impact will this have?

If the impact is similar to smartphones, then it can be treated as the next step. People will be checking their messages without using their phone. Directions can flash on the screen, not buzz in the pocket. Calls and meetings can be seamless. Cameras snap life moments. The glasses would accompany the lives of people more intimately than a phone sitting in a drawer.

This intimate connection continues many people's perpetual reliance on checking social media consistently. The blend of social and life becomes warped when there is a virtual overlay over the world around people. Once the virtual and real mix, as it does now, would people turn back?

This is all extrapolation based on current trends on mobile use. Comparing current trends with future innovations is unwise. The comparisons are comfortable, though it can quickly turn false. Time will tell.

Before we leave AR glasses, I want to touch on one great area of use – for the hearing-impaired.

The National Theatre has launched smart caption glasses for the hearing impaired, displaying subtitles during a theatrical production. Accenture, Epson's Moverio BT-350 glasses, and Action on Hearing Loss UK assisted with the project.

The glasses display a transcript of the production, updated live as the performance goes on. The technology senses at what point the play is at, then flash the relevant subtitles on the lens.

Earlier today I tried out the glasses in a 15-minute excerpt of *Exit the King*. The smart caption glasses sit comfortably and show hovering text. The subtitles also come with who is talking, select stage directions, and sound effects. There was a slight bit of lag, as the technology recognises what part of the play it was currently on. Overall, my views are very positive; it is a revolutionary piece of kit which will help those in need. Users can rent smart caption glasses at the National Theatre.

Then during the Q&A session afterwards, Lisa Burger, Executive Director at the National Theatre, highlighted that the glasses are part of the company's drive to improve accessibility. The Director looks forward to their more extensive use, 'not only at the NT, but in the entertainment industry more widely.'

What is interesting as well was Dave Finch, a vital member of the testing group. Having reached early retirement, he was suddenly struck by hearing loss and, driven by his experiences, sought to help others with the same impairment.

After making some light-hearted jokes about speaking to an all-journalist theatre, Dave went into more detail: 'The one thing that has struck me is that it's almost impossible to describe their impact to a 'normal' hearing person. For someone hard of hearing, they represent the difference between being able to go to the theatre whenever you choose and staying away.

'Quite a lot of deaf people don't realise what is out there to help them or haven't even contemplated that an evening at the theatre is possible, but these glasses represent a fantastic step forward.'

The smart caption glasses apply directly to using AR for good causes. Hearing loss is becoming commonplace across the country. Action on Hearing Loss UK estimates that around 1 in 6 people have hearing loss in the United Kingdom, rising to 1 in 5 by 2035. So the NT sought to improve their accessibility in light of these statistics and their company strategy.[32]

The technology impressed as well. Experts from Accenture Extended Reality worked to refine the smart glasses user interface, with around six months of testing. The team built the project using the Epson Moverio BT-350 smart glasses, developed specifically with arts and culture applications in mind. Any performance can use the smart caption glasses. Further, the Accenture representative noted that the glasses had been tested with more improvised gigs as well.

The glasses are functional, the text is clear, and I can see its applications being beneficial. The NT will likely use the glasses for years to come – as they should. And it provides a benchmark of other ways which the specs will change a culture.

---

[32] Facts and Figures. https://www.actiononhearingloss.org.uk/about-us/our-research-and-evidence/facts-and-figures/. Accessed 24 Feb. 2020.

TRAINING: TRAINING THE NEXT GENERATION OF EMPLOYEES SAFELY

I shall be blunt. From healthcare to aeroplanes, companies used immersive technologies to train people in many, many ways. In the future, more investment will lead to more companies adopting both VR and AR. Why? Because it works, and I cannot stress how much our lives will change over the next few decades because of it.

Numerous scientific studies have shown that virtual reality training helps users learn new skills. One piece of research in 2018 found that immersive training is an inexpensive and effective way to teach fire prevention among professionals.[33] Another study in 2018, from the University of Illinois, covers how it can help improve patient safety and learn sophisticated surgery skills. The technology can also provide detailed reports on the trainee's performance, which instructors can implement as part of evaluations at the end of sessions.[34] One more study, from the University of Copenhagen, explored which scenarios VR headsets can help with learning. The study identified various useful attributes, such as understanding spatial and visual information, scanning or observational

---

[33] Sankaranarayanan, Ganesh, et al. "Immersive Virtual Reality-Based Training Improves Response in a Simulated Operating Room Fire Scenario." Surgical Endoscopy, vol. 32, no. 8, Aug. 2018, pp. 3439–49. Springer Link, doi:10.1007/s00464-018-6063-x.

[34] McGuire, Laura Stone, and Ali Alaraj. "Competency Assessment in Virtual Reality-Based Simulation in Neurosurgical Training." Comprehensive Healthcare Simulation: Neurosurgery, edited by Ali Alaraj, Springer International Publishing, 2018, pp. 153–57. Springer Link, doi:10.1007/978-3-319-75583-0_12.

skills, and controlling emotional responses to stressful situations.[35]

The study also identified cases where virtual reality training failed, including motion sickness and distractions. Like with all training methods, each one needs to be applied with different objectives in mind.

These experiences work because they bring people into the virtual environment. Jessica Driscoll, Head of immersive at Digital Catapult, argues that the environment can influence behavior: 'It's not only interactive CGI simulation VR experiences that can be transformative in a training environment, the use of 360 3D film creates a compelling and memorable experience in a training setting. While in the role of VR Director of Development at Cornerstone I witnessed a huge range of behaviour and reactions in users ranging from teachers to social workers, prison wardens to politicians post-viewing. Being put in the shoes of a child while they experienced trauma from the womb through to a toxic environment where no child should be was an intervention that you simply could not achieve any other way and created a lasting impact on the users.'

Anyone can use most VR headsets as there are many sorts of training modules. Both the Oculus Rift S and HTC Vive Pro are high-end headsets with 6DoF controllers, meaning people can interact with their environments. They also let people walk around the area to

---

[35] Jensen, Lasse, and Flemming Konradsen. "A Review of the Use of Virtual Reality Head-Mounted Displays in Education and Training." Education and Information Technologies, vol. 23, no. 4, July 2018, pp. 1515–29. Springer Link, doi:10.1007/s10639-017-9676-0.

interact with virtual objects. In short, they are perfect for high-end experiences.

The standalone Oculus Go, alongside other mobile headsets, have less usability as functionality is either 3DoF, or nonexistent. These headsets can provide a small level of interactivity, but it is not as extensive as other ones available. That said, they can display 360 videos on a topic, giving an immersive experience.

All headsets have their pros and cons, though it depends on the goal. Does the business need employees to handle precise controls? Or merely an immersive way of learning new concepts?

At its core, the technology gives a more hands-on feel. Learning about cooking from a book is one way; chopping virtual bananas is another. Reading about the body is helpful, but seeing the inside adds depth to the learning experience.

As an example, mentioned briefly, VR is good for learning spatial information. If training to be a surgeon, and it provides haptic feedback with 6DoF freedom, then it helps to teach where organs are and how to cut them. Teachers can find it challenging to deliver spatial knowledge with just words. As an example, Immerse worked with QinetiQ to provide VR submarine training to help lower the costs of training (one of my favorite examples I have seen).

On top of these, Oxford VR created an automated VR treatment that delivers psychological therapy via a computer-generated virtual coach or avatar. The results of the research, which focused its attention on fear of heights, were published in the Lancet Psychiatry publication, receiving global acclaim. While rigorous testing will be vital going forward, Oxford VR has broken new ground in 2018 by proving the effective use of automated VR therapy to treat mental health disorders.

Many skills can be trained with virtual reality. Like all learning methods, some are better than others, depending on the situation. Many people feel motion sickness in the tech. Losing a sense of self, some people find the dissonance between real life and the virtual world sickening. It is a fair and common criticism. But over time, as hardware improves, the issue will lessen.

Sam Watts, Director of Immersive Technologies at Make Real, has his own thoughts on the topic:

'VR training or within virtual environment simulators isn't anything new but until a few years ago, it was reserved for specialist sectors where clear cost-savings were more obvious, like full flight simulators being cheaper, and considerably safer for all involved, than putting untrained pilots into real planes. However these simulators still cost millions to deploy, operate and maintain, often only replicating one specific cockpit or plane, requiring multiple units individually configured for training at scale. On the software side, simulation databases were often clunky, old engines with costly recurring subscriptions to keep alive. Therefore they had to be in operation 24/7 in order to ensure return of investment and value to organisations.

'However with the release of the Oculus Rift in 2016 and a range of increasingly higher specification VR headsets since then, like the HTC Vive Pro and Varjo VR2, visual fidelity and accuracy of simulations has increased proportionately to the capabilities of the 3D games engines powering the experiences, alongside considerable reduction in costs of creating the content and deploying the hardware. What used to cost £20,000+ for a headset with lesser specifications can be matched with far superior capabilities for less than £1,000.

'As a result, more organisations are embracing immersive technologies like VR and AR to incorporate into their employee training across a much wider set of sectors and use cases, especially in and around the scenarios associated with health, safety and well-being. VR allows employees to train in realistic simulated environments with full interaction metrics, feedback and dynamic scenarios controlled by instructors but ultimately, fail safely within consistent, repeatable mechanisms, without interruption to organisational operations or personal danger to other employees.

'This isn't to say it is the magic bullet to replace all types of training prior to VR, rather an additional tool to add to the learners toolkit to enhance and tackle specific areas where traditional e-learning or face-to-face methods have struggled to prove value. This could be allowing pilots to train to a base level of knowledge of the layout of a cockpit and essential safety procedures that can be completed outside of the full flight simulator, reducing operational pressure and costs on the high demands of the systems previously, which do not necessarily need to be carried out in a full physical replica.

'These 'hard skills' are also fairly obvious uses of VR, where muscle memory, interactions with simulated assets and suchlike are a logical choice of training scenario. What is becoming more apparent through academic research and organisations working with considerate studios, is that other use cases around behavioural change, communications and making us better humans are also viable topics to train in - whilst not directly related to immediate safety in an obvious sense, if we can work together whilst looking out for one another, the workplaces of the future become safer overall, no matter their purpose.'

I thank Sam Watts for his contribution.

The experience is also very distracting. Powering through a blood vein in VR to see how the body works is cool, but perhaps not for learning. People can get swept away by the experience, meaning they retain less exact knowledge like with the flashcard method.

As one example, Virgin Atlantic introduced immersive training technology, as part of a collaboration with SITA – that allows the airline's cabin crew to use AR to familiarise themselves with new aircraft. Using an iOS app, cabin crew use AR to walk through the layout of Virgin Atlantic's Boeing 787 Dreamliner aircraft, without taking a peek in real life. The experience complements the existing classroom-based training, and the app allows crew members to see the cabin projected as a portal, which they can walk into. The AR app simulates the full-size view of the interior cabin, giving the crew a feel for their new working environment, including accurate spatial awareness.

Don Langford, CIO of Virgin Atlantic, said: 'Today innovation is the lifeblood of a modern airline. New technologies such as augmented reality hold out the promise to better manage our airline operations while providing an enriched experience to our increasingly tech-savvy passengers. SITA has long been a partner in exploring the frontiers of technology and this AR application is no exception.'

As another example, Medical Realities is a team offering medical training products, utilising immersive technologies. By using the Oculus Rift and Google Cardboard, the company designs experiences for medical students learning more about people's bodies. The team can record 360 videos in 4K, so medical students can get a good view of what is happening. While this is different from virtual reality, it still offers an immersive experience so students can feel like they are in the environment. The platform also comes with a test, to best understand how well someone is doing. As a learning tool, it is an effective way of learning new skills and, vitally, check whether it works.

Various military organisations have adopted virtual reality. It is used alongside other training methods for countries such as the USA and is a part of their overall training as soldiers and expert engineers. Microsoft signed a $400 million deal with the US army to use mixed-reality headsets during training.[36] Some USA personnel use a VR trainer to simulate jumps from the air before they leap. The

---

[36] Kelly, Makena. "Microsoft Secures $480 Million HoloLens Contract from US Army." The Verge, 28 Nov. 2018, https://www.theverge.com/2018/11/28/18116939/microsoft-army-hololens-480-million-contract-magic-leap.

approach lets them conduct tests on drops over and over again, to ensure perfection.

Much like education in classrooms, virtual reality training has been happening for many years. While tracking systems used augmented reality for decades, innovators have found new ways of using the tech in wider industries. The difference over the last few years is that enterprise-grade devices are more easily accessed with a flow of capital to back innovators.

Some headsets are different. In a virtual environment, new skills can be taught and learned with time. Controllers actively interact with environments, safely and securely where trainers use the data to make improvements. Augmented reality can do the same as employees get to grips with new situations.

And in the future? Nick Rosa, Global Head of Immersive Learning at Accenture, gives his thoughts: 'One area I find particularly interesting is the use of VR to train robotic processes. By tracking how people complete tasks in a virtual environment, the data can then be used to improve machines who can learn from their successes and mistakes via ML. In this way we train the machines of the future to perform tasks that could be at human risk, such as loss of limbs or falling from heights. It's the blend of VR and ML which could significantly revolutionise industry.'

Virtual reality training will likely continue to prosper in the future. The future is now and will continue to evolve as the years roll by.

MOVIES: A NEW WAY TO WATCH ENTERTAINMENT

Virtual reality movies are the culmination of many years of experimentation and evolution. In the late 1920s, the film industry was revolutionised by the introduction of sound with movies, or talkies. Now we see a repeat of this phenomenon with VR films.

Initially with *The Jazz Singer* (1927), continued by *All Quiet on the Western Front* (1930), and parodied in *Singin' in the Rain* (1952), audio began to transform film. It was a time of rudimentary transition, restricted camera movements, live dialogue, and minimal editing. The earliest talkies were primitive, designed to capitalise on the novelty of sound. Talkies eventually dominated the filmmaking landscape – after extensive exploration and experimentation.

The VR industry is filled with gimmicks and improper use of the tech as companies once again cash in on the novelty, or fail to capitalise upon the potential assets. It is an exciting time and will give birth to influential companies in much the same way that Warner Brothers was born from the talkies era.

Now, virtual reality movies are immersive experiences where viewers can watch a film with a VR headset. A fair few VR headsets enable anyone to watch any film. However, there is a difference between virtual reality movies and 360 videos. Virtual reality is when players can move and interact in a virtual environment. 360 videos are passive viewing experiences similar to YouTube videos, but not within a virtual space. Some virtual reality movies can only be used on high-end headsets with interactable elements. The videos do not let the viewers interact, yet they have a powerful impact because of their immersion.

Most people use terms like virtual reality and 360 videos synonymously, to mean the same thing. For the sake of simplicity, I shall also do the same.

Sol Rogers, CEO and Founder of REWIND, has his own thoughts: 'It's not just the film industry that is using immersive technology to engage. The world of theatre is also experimenting with these new mediums. While the theater has been using all sorts of effects—from lighting to sound—for hundreds of years to make the audience experience more immersive, new pioneering technologies offer a unique way of adding an extra dimension to performances.

'Technology can also engage a younger demographic to whom the theatre may not be immediately appealing. In addition, VR can make the theatre more accessible—by putting 360-degree videos online, many more people can be exposed to this form of entertainment.'

When exploring the topic, one event I must mention is Raindance. Each year, the event consistently shows the very best content, and I look forward to it every year. So it seems right and proper to talk about them.

The Curious Tale of the Stolen Pets

Created by Fast Travel Games, *The Curious Tale of the Stolen Pets* is a departure from *Budget Cuts* and *Budget Cuts 2* with no stabbing present. It is also a departure from the previous experience of members from the team, as they came from titles like *Battlefield*. Nice.

Instead, it is a cute game where the user plays the role of a child being guided through their memories, as a homely grandfather narrates their past life. The aim is to solve the mystery of the stolen pets, as they can be found anywhere on a floating rock in the sky. By using the controllers, the world can be rotated and interacted with, to find the cute critters in bushes or trees.

Cute and warm-hearted, the game felt fantastic to play. It was easy to feel lost navigating through the virtual world, solving puzzles and finding new hidden things to see. I was also stumped by one problem involving a teapot; I was slightly ashamed, but I chuckled regardless.

If you own a 6DoF headset (Oculus Quest, Oculus Rift S, PlayStation VR, HTC Vive for example), *The Curious Tale of the Stolen Pets* is worth a go.

Doctor Who: The Edge of Time

HTC invited us to try *Doctor Who: The Edge of Time* in a pop-up in East London, before heading to Raindance Immersive. The team warmly welcomed us to try a shortened demo of the experience, using the Vive Cosmos.

As per usual, the Doctor got herself in a bit of an issue by being trapped somewhere. You play yourself, standing in a TARDIS and being guided by the Doctor to various locations to help free her from her entrapment and, hopefully, save the universe.

According to Marcus Moresby, the team worked closely with the BBC to work out what creatures can and cannot be used. He also watched hours upon hours of the show to pinpoint what makes up the heart of the show, to integrate it into the gameplay.

We had fun fiddling about with the TARDIS controls, wandering across a dark world, and solving puzzles. Like with the other game, we also got stuck on a simple problem, and we were slightly annoyed with ourselves afterwards. This isn't the fault of the game; we were just very, very stupid.

If you are a fan, *Doctor Who: The Edge of Time* is a great experience to play.

Anonymous

Anonymous is a powerful 360 narrative film telling the personal recollection of a child of an alcoholic mother. The experience is twelve minutes long, though it was an intense twelve minutes.

Samantha Kingston, a talented creative, tells her story about growing up with her mother and all the things she did while staying at home. She explored small details like fumbling for the keys for slightly longer just so she can delay the time before coming into the house. She also told about how she knew all the hiding places of the alcohol, and how her mother filled them with water to see if she would continue the game further.

Samantha Kingston, creator of *Anonymous*, said the project 'is a passion project that was built upon a tragedy using my experience of grief and loss, bringing together what we have learned from the industry. I felt the best way to share the story was through a 360-narrative piece.

Because of the taboo subject of alcoholism, I used immersive tech because as people typically shy away from the topic in real life—but with 360, you cannot turn away from something that must be discussed more.'

Five chairs encircle the person, who is directly being told the story as though Samantha is telling her mother in person. Each chair represents the five stages of grief. And occasionally, Samantha appears in another chair to highlight another point about her life.

Anonymous is an incredibly intense and powerful film from Raindance Immersive. The film also uses the medium in a meaningful and impactful way. It provides a compelling experience in a way that is more intense than cinema can be. Considering it was made with a crowdfunded budget of £2,000, it is an astonishing piece to watch.

Playing God

Playing God is an interactive sci-fi drama that presents the player with several difficult morality choices. Piloting a ship, players judge whether refugees can come onto a ship that already has stretched supplies.

On paper, the experience is an expansion on the philosophy of lifeboat ethics, only with spaceships. In practice, Ben Fredericks and Alex Rühl use visual tricks to put you in the role of the captain, with computer panels and beaming in holograms for additional insights. It's a lot of fun while being through-provoking as well.

It is also a branching storyline, where difference choices bring about different conclusions. We wish we had more time to try out different endings, but it is great to see the absolute replay value of what can be done.

Playing God is an engaging and fun experience which is excellent to discuss afterwards, as different people would have different opinions on the choices that can be made. It's well worth a play for anyone interested in sci-fi and philosophy. The potential sequel, based on genetically modifying children, is eagerly anticipated.

Afterlife

Afterlife shows the story of family members as they deal with the death of their recently deceased child. After a tragic accident, it follows each family member as they deal with the situation. From a mother who is convinced he is still alive, to a father who wants to leave the house that reminds him of the accident.

Like *Playing God*, *Afterlife* has multiple paths and endings, but instead of clicking on certain items, it is based on where the player focuses. For example, if the player watches the father, it continues the story from the father's perspective. This then leads to a path which is different from the others, until they connect again at specific points.

The idea of a story based on focus, rather than selecting options, is revolutionary. Instead of explicitly choosing options on a list after pondering for some time, the player's focus on the story becomes the driver of choices. We had not seen anything like it before, and it is genius to see in action.

The film is fantastic, and we really look forward to watching it again to see what else the story brings.

Rise of Animals

This was the first Magic Leap One experience which Raindance Immersive has ever done, and it is a great one to start with. *Rise of Animals* is a truly unique experience that really brings to light the power of immersive content for engagement.

Imagine standing in a designed room with pieces of paper on the walls, a desk, and pot plants peeking out. Then, imagine selecting a creature and watching it walk, fly, or swim around a room. All the while, Sir David Attenborough talks about the beast at hand. From soaring overhead to swimming behind pillars, it provides a fantastic way to learn more about the natural world.

It makes us think about how it can be used in education as a powerful way to learn new concepts. Take biology. Reading about it can work or watching it on TV. Virtual reality can bring people through the human body. But the Magic Leap One has the potential to put creatures in a room in real-life and watch them soar past. That is a powerful way to learn something new.

Rise of Animals may be challenging to see as it uses a Magic Leap One in a designed location. But if you have the chance, be sure to check it out.

Drip Drop

Drip Drop is a trippy experience which highlights the unheard voices of filmmakers. The user is situated in an underwater void, with the floating ghosts of people around them. By blinking, the apparitions form over time to then tell their story.

The theme of the experience is attention. The more care you give, the more that the voices are heard and given form. By looking away, the voice silences itself. In this way, the theme is that underrepresented voices can come to the surface to break the surface.

Drip Drop is a unique experience from Raindance Immersive that is well worth a go.

The Holy City

One of the most visually impressive experiences at Raindance Immersive, *The Holy City* is a narrative experienced based on Jerusalem.

There are several versions of the experience, but the shortened version has two parts. One is the VR-run setup where users navigate through stunning photogrammetric recreations of locations such as the Holy Sepulchre. The other is a series of puzzles solved on a tablet, which people can work together on.

What struck me was the impact and power of wandering through the locations. Jerusalem is on the bucket list, but seeing the site recreated in such detail was incredibly impactful. Its sheer size, beauty and religious significance were humbling to see.

The creator hopes to bridge barriers between faiths with the piece. We hope so as well.

With films and virtual reality, the crucial difference is the role of the viewer. Will McMaster, Head of VR at Visualise, highlights that the viewer is taking up physical space within the virtual world: 'I think the sensation of watching a story in VR is as much a physical experience as it is visual... in traditional media, we don't have to take physical space into account because the viewer never changes physical position.

They're always in a chair, watching a two-dimensional representation of reality. In VR, we are changing the viewer's entire sense of reality.'

'It sounds really obvious, but it's something I think about a lot because you start to realise that your entire set of advantages and limitations in telling a story in VR stem from this physicality... I don't think these disadvantages mean that you can't tell a great story in VR, but I do think that how that great story is told is going to be very different from how it's done in traditional media.'

At the most basic level, the viewer has a place in a new world. While cuts and camera movements guide films audiences, their identity is separate. There is no need to give the audience a role.

VR challenges this. When placed in a virtual world, the viewer feels that they have a physicality and presence within it. Viewers start to question their identity among the fuss and furor.

So what techniques are pioneered for the medium?

The team at BBC Research and Development are currently exploring VR, experimenting with various techniques and applications. After a short while Alia Sheikh, filmmaker at BBC R&D, found there was a solution within traditional theatre. 'Consider a traditional theatre production which deals with audience members –

viewers – that observe from a fixed location, who are only ever seeing a wide angle view and who have independent control over where to look.

'There are obvious commonalities with VR and 360 experiences. We found that members of a theatre troupe are expert at directing attention across a field of view by using sound, lighting and visual cues, and an understanding of group behavior – using their own attention to direct the audiences. It's these sorts of cues we need to be using in VR experiences. If every other person in a 360 scene looks to the left, in the direction of a sound cue, chances are, your viewer will look in that direction as well. But instead of the action feeling forced, it becomes natural, as if the viewer is discovering things for themselves.'[37]

Here, Alia draws parallels between a play production and VR. Virtual reality movies must subtly direct the viewer's attention in the story, the same way a play might. If out of sight, a person is also out of mind – until they move, and they then become a point of attention. This cannot be shown with camera cuts or flashes, as they have to become a natural part of the scene.

Other companies use immersive theatre as a term. Aardman used these same techniques in the production of *We Wait*. Aardman collaborated with the BBC to collect the stories of migrants, and illustrated their flight during the refugee crisis. *We Wait* follows a Syrian family

---

[37] Ffiske, Tom. "'Paint Me a Scene': How Is VR Storytelling Different?" Virtual Perceptions, 9 Nov. 2016, https://www.virtualperceptions.com/paint-me-a-scene-how-is-vr-storytelling-different/.

about to embark on their second attempt to cross the sea to Greece.

Daniel Efergan, Digital Group Creative Director at Aardman, understands how the viewer personally connects to the experience. 'With this piece we were interested in how the connection between our characters and their stories could be interlocked with the audience, in particular using eye contact and other social interactions to drive greater emotional connection. This was a chance to play with these situations, understand how they can be used to drive the story forward.[38]

'When we were forming this narrative the press was full of stories around 'the migrant crisis', as it was dubbed, but we felt the coverage offered simplified views, gathered facts but ultimately a homogenous point of view that didn't deal with the multifaceted issues, the wealth of wants, fears, and feelings of the many individuals affected by what was going on. We hoped by telling a few personal stories we could add a little more to this important conversation.'

In *We Wait*, being shouted at and blinded by headlights makes a mark on the viewer. It occurs while being restricted to a single spot, making the viewer feel helpless. The abstract models added to the experience. By taking a less realistic approach, the production felt emotionally charged, or rawer. A sense of place also contributed to the story's engagement. As Daniel said, 'a simple glance from another character seemed enough to draw the audience closer, more likely to follow a character's story.'

---

[38] Ibid

These sentiments are mirrored by *Ctrl*, the world's first long-form virtual reality drama which gave the viewer a specific role. In *Ctrl*, the viewer watches the last round of an e-sports tournament. The events take place in a virtual arena. They have front-row seats to the action and can see into the player's world through webcam-style screens around the stadium. Because the audience feels like they are watching a tournament, they become part of the narrative.[39]

I was fortunate enough to see the production myself during its launch. The production allowed a level of emotional investment which linked the viewer to the story. Virtual reality movies allow viewers to feel a sense of presence unparalleled by traditional media, and *Ctrl* capitalised on that unique feeling.

Viewers felt emotionally drained and shocked by the end. Virtual reality movies play tricks on the mind and can be far harsher than watching television. Similarly, YouTube is full of content creators playing horror video games, and they cite that there is no parallel. For horror games, VR always wins.

Any genre can fit into VR even something as banal as a cooking show would be more intuitive if you're stood by the host watching them cook. Virtual reality movies are not limited to particular genres, though some types may require more creativity in application than others.

The VR experiences may, therefore, go beyond what some minds can endure. Kate Gray, a videogames journalist developing her own game, is both fascinated by VR and terrified of its capabilities:

---

[39] ibid

'Our brains have no way to process something that looks very, very real, but won't hurt us, so the only thing it can do is go through the motions as if it were real. That means anxiety, panic attacks, and heightened adrenalin levels, which are all the things that are unpleasant and potentially dangerous for our bodies to handle. It's not like a rollercoaster, because there's some level of trust in the underlying mechanics that the ride won't break. Virtual reality movies are different as they're entirely immersive, so we forget that level of confidence.

'So I foresee a couple of stories about horror games taking it too far. That's a boundary that people will want to push, and with a medium that's really, really new and incredibly interesting, I don't blame those devs for wanting to see what the platform is capable of, I'm just wary of that, mostly coming from the experience I've had some anxiety attacks. I wouldn't wish that on anyone!' Such concerns should be taken into consideration.'[40]

Evangelists may discuss how the technology will revolutionise how we consume media – but few currently explore how it may be too immersive as some may not be able to cope with heightened adrenaline or anxiety. There can be, realistically, too much of a good thing.

Others do not even mention the sheer amount of work behind a production. Peter Collis is a veteran producer in the immersive industry. After being Head of Camera Systems at Inition, Mr Collis now freelances for a few organisations, including Philharmonia. I caught wind of a

---

[40] ibid

great story from one of his recent projects, which I felt should be retold. The story gives a great insight into the technical side of immersive recordings, as well as what can be done if something goes wrong (and promptly saved by the skills of the team):

'Following the success of The Virtual Orchestra and Beethoven 5 VR pieces, Philharmonia wanted to capture in 360 the last part of Mahler's 9th Symphony, being performed at the South Bank Centre. It was also going out as a live transmission on YouTube, as one of the first live broadcasts of its kind. The sound was to be captured and recorded by the combination of a few groups. On previous occasions, we'd recorded the audio with binaural mics just from the camera positions. For Mahler, the whole Orchestra was to be locally mic'd up so that a full clean Ambisonic mix could be created for a location-based, multiple speaker experience.

'My job was to do the 360-filming bit. Every 360-filming job I've done I've pushed to be stereoscopic, it gives a richness that I don't think is there in mono. So, we got hold of a Jump rig and I added a top camera to capture the ceiling. The Jump is an array of 16 GoPros set in a rig around 30cm in diameter. It normally has a bit of a hole top and bottom, but we were keen to have a complete 360 space for the viewer to explore in. It also comes with a recommended minimum near object distance of 1.5m… Which was a problem. The Mahler piece requires a full orchestra of over 100 players crammed on the relatively tight Royal Festival Stage. Where we wanted to place the camera was only a few cms from the closest players.

'As DOP I had to make the call… It either is not going to work because musicians are too close to camera or we squeeze them all back away enough for it to work, or even 'drop' some of the players (which no one was going to love me for). We re-jiggled the staging and pushed the players back, but they all need their elbow room to wield their violin and cello bows… And it wasn't enough. So we asked the unthinkable and said can we drop 4 or so players to make it work…

'I wasn't invited to the meeting between the lead conductor, festival director, promotions dept and the like. But the outcome was they gave me the reduced numbers. So, we set up a test day, tweaked the auditorium lighting, mapped the space for the audio.

'The day came, and we were ready – bar one worry. The system did not have a wired start trigger, it was a WiFi-based system. The bit of the performance we wanted was right at the end. The rig was prone to overheating when running continuously so we couldn't just capture the whole performance. The WiFi trigger worked perfectly fine in the empty auditorium but (through previous experience) I knew that when 2000 people and their WiFi-enabled phones, were in the venue that wasn't necessarily going to be the case.

'So, my next tricky demand: I needed a seat in the front row so that if I couldn't trigger the system remotely, I'd have to jump up on stage to fire it manually. Again, they agreed (also saying let's hope that isn't necessary). The piece is incredibly demanding on the players and especially the conductor so there are short breaks in the 90-minute performance, so we identified the opportune moment for me to jump on stage should I need to. And of course, I did!

'So, the rig was recording, I sat back and hoped it wouldn't overheat. It didn't. We got the shot. It was a pig to stitch, all those bows and stitch lines (in 3D too remember). But it got done and is out there.'

So far, we have explored how virtual reality movies affect us. But films themselves are not going anywhere. They are a great form of entertainment, journalism, and art which will not be taken over by new mediums. Instead, VR films will likely continue to form their niche. Stories best told in an immersive way will continue to flourish, while the blockbusters keep the cash rolling.

There are times and places for VR films, particularly with storytelling. It isn't a competition between mainstream movies and an upbeat new medium. Both will grow and be used depending on the tale to tell. All these examples all come together in some fascinating conclusions on how to tell stories through VR. Aardman, the BBC, and Breaking Fourth, among others, have all identified theatre techniques as a solid base for production.

Muki Kulhan, CIO of Muki-International, sees the area expanding quickly: 'There's a lot of immersive awards happening, and… I would love to see more charts in the future.'[41]

---

[41] "Future of Storytelling : More immersive and interactive experiences Muki Kulhan GameChangers London" YouTube.
https://www.youtube.com/watch?v=klOa41Tm0Ko. Accessed 24 Feb. 2020.

By inspecting how actors on a stage direct the viewer's attention – movement, sounds, glances – the companies are finding ways to move the viewer's head to where they want. VR is intrinsically different from films. It is not a passive square to be watched, but an immersive production where the rules change. Visualise correctly identified this distinction and applied it to their works, while Kate Gray points out that this feeling of immersion may be too much to some. A VR comedy show was the worst example of VR that I have seen – no engagement, or purpose, just merely an exploitation of a gimmick. VR goes beyond simple tricks towards artistic complexity.

At the beginning of this chapter, I cited comparisons to the sound revolution in the film industry. We are in the Wild West, using new technology and finding ways to maximise its potential. VR is in the same role, and there is no doubt that the revolution shall come to an end. Probably with a bang and a Warner Brothers equivalent arising in a few years. The question is one of application, and how these experiments in VR storytelling shall develop.

INTERVIEW: DEEP DIVE INTO IMMERSIVE FILM

VR and 360 filmmaking is a very different process compared to traditional TV and cinema, and with it comes the baggage of learning new techniques for filming. Previously I described 2016 as the 'Wild West' period of the industry where there are less rules, and filmmaking techniques were less established. The new, somewhat untraveled land forced some filmmakers to learn new tricks on the fly, adapting to the situations they want to portray.

One of the people researching the field is Alia Sheikh, a Senior Development Producer in BBC Research and Development, who experiments to find out what works and what doesn't. In a 360-degree field, a viewer can look wherever they like; Alia's technical research covers the psychological techniques broadcasters can use to push viewers in the right direction subtly.

To Alia, these subtle ways of directing the viewer can work in a number of ways: a voice to the left of the scene; the people at the center of the scene pointing to the left; or a person walking across the scene towards the left, among many other dynamic prods. Producers can make the same effect with light – like moths to a flame, and viewers tend to follow the source of light over dark.

Producers lift these ideas from traditional theatre techniques, and with gaze-tracking software, Alia noticed how effective they could be for viewers in 360°. Even then, Alia found that some people still tend to dart around the scene left and right, not focusing on a particular area for a long time. These viewers like to scan their surroundings as a scene plays along, rather than stare at one area for a long time. Others might choose one area of interest and remain fixed on it until very strongly directed to shift attention. People don't stop being highly individual.

Scene transitions can still happen, and they do not need to be complicated. Fade to black then fading into a new scene still works, for example, and this matches the use of lighting effects in theatrical productions. Not unexpectedly, spinning the camera into a new view tends to make people feel nauseated, however, if the footage is sped up fast enough the motion blur effects disappear and turn into a more acceptable 'blinking' effect which surprisingly sometimes works for transitions.

Level of viewer engagement can be affected by the amount the viewer can be included in the scene. Alia created a scene when two people were arguing, with the viewer listening in, and then an almost identical scene except, in this case, the people arguing attempted to involve the viewer. There was far less engagement when the viewer remained unacknowledged.

Although in the second example, the actors in the scene attempted to draw the viewer into the scene, the viewer was not able to affect the scene in any way. But when the viewer was given a name and brought into the argument – with frequent side glances from the arguers towards the viewer – attention spiked upwards. The Viewer became a part of the discussion, not just a passive listener. Alia calls this the 'illusion of interaction.'

Another factor is the distance from the camera, and how it affects the watcher. Alia staged a fight between two people, and situated the camera 2ft, 3ft, and 4ft away from the fight. What Alia found was that the viewer's level of comfort is somewhat contingent to the distances of real life. If an argument was two feet away, viewers felt overwhelmed, whereas if a fight was 4ft away, they felt safer watching the conflict. Distance, in this case, affected the emotional impact of the scene, and the 'correct' range for the camera from the actors depended on the desired emotional state for the viewer as well as taking into account that the low resolution of current 360° systems makes it hard to see people clearly if they are too far away.

The team found that changing the distance of scene objects from the camera also allows them to play with size using traditional perspective effects very convincingly. Working with the Familia De La Noche team on their 2016 production of *Gullivers Travels*, Alia and Trainee R&D Engineer Sam Nicholson, found that it was possible to approximate a 'giant' talking to 'Lilliputians'. The giant effect was created by placing one actor on a stepladder and having him lean forward over the 360° camera which had been placed close between his hands. The Lilliputians were created by having the actors a few meters from the camera, looking artificially 'up' at the giant (whom himself exaggerating his gaze downwards). There is a perception that a 360° camera perspective is somehow a more 'honest' representation of the world, as the entire panorama can be viewed and there is no hidden area 'behind' the camera. However, these tests do show that the camera can, as was always the case, very effectively lie.

When the team went to the Edinburgh Fringe and did experiments filming street performers, they found the same conclusions – camera position is vital. There is a perfect middle between performer and audience where a viewer can watch the performance without being part of a crowd, and therefore be in an excellent position to observe both. This position only really makes sense if it is either essential for the viewer to be able to turn away from the performer and see the crowd for some reason, or if being situated at the front of the group would offer a poor view of the performance. Once the action is even a few meters away, on current playback hardware, the detail is lost, and in that instance, it is preferable to move the camera closer to the performance at the expense of feeling 'part of' an audience.

For one-on-one performances, however, where the viewer is the only audience member, more interesting camera positions afford in one case, for example, having a performer juggle over the camera to make the viewer look up and feel a sense of peril, as well as provide an alternative view. In another example, a performer thrust a flaming sword near the camera and gave a cheeky smile, a look that is closer to what the viewer would experience during a one-on-one interaction. These performances were made accessible via an experimental BBC R&D's WebVR player, and used on the BBC TASTER site to give an impression of the variety of street performances on show at the Edinburgh Festival.

Crucially, having a bespoke player to contain all the content meant that content did not have to be made available as individual clips via an external platform, and the way that audiences navigated around the player (either on a headset or non-headset device) could be customised to the content on offer.

From arguing friends to talking giants to dancers at the Fringe – at the heart of it all is narrative. No good story works solely on structure – it needs a tale to weave it together. And after much tinkering on her side, Alia came away with three key questions that any 360° experience producer needs to be able to answer:

1. Who is the audience? What is their role?
2. How do you want to make them feel?
3. What do you want them to know/understand?

Overall, Alia is excited about the future. 'The language of filmmaking is still there; it's just in a different dialect.'[42]

AR CREATORS: A NEW CHANNEL FOR MARKETING

When any new industry flourishes, job roles pop into existence as well. Careers which did not exist several years ago - developers, immersive producers - are created to help companies develop and grow. One that has come out of nowhere is the rise of AR for marketing, and the creators who help.

The topic is massive, covering everything in movies, retail, packaging, and much more. We can talk all day on the campaigns and launches which appear all the

---

[42] More information on the research can be found in this excellent paper: Sheikh, A., et al. Directing Attention in 360-Degree Video. Jan. 2016, pp. 29 (9 .)-29 (9 .). digital-library.theiet.org, doi:10.1049/ibc.2016.0029.

time. But behind every campaign and tool are the people who make the tools themselves, and the way they develop for their clients.

Why now? Why has AR face filters risen in use over the last couple of years, and how are brands capitalising on the new trend? The answer connects to Stories on Instagram, Snapchat, and Facebook, and the influence they have on friends and family. Other innovations, such as WebAR, dramatically increase the potential audience of a product. Together, over the last few years, some budding entrepreneurs who capitalise on the trend and, over time, soared to massive popularity. AR is a wide-open area, which covers everything from retail to packaging. Marketing is no different; as a creative industry, there are all sorts of ways which companies use the technology.

For example, when PUMA launched its flagship New York store in 2019, Alternative Genius used Zappar's tool ZapWorks to create a WebAR experience. By scanning tags with their cameras, shoppers can then interact with the basketball line of trainers in the store.

The most exciting innovation in this area is WebAR, which lets anyone with a mobile device scan a code and launch an AR experience hosted on a webpage. The change vastly expands the number of people who can use AR without needing to download an app - so much so that I would not be surprised if I see more brands use the technology this year. The potential is more extensive when it includes packaging as well. Imagine picking up a drink and scanning with a phone to find out more information. The process can be seamless.

Tools like ZapWorks are easy to get to grips with. When I learned how to use the platform, it took me an hour to have Bulbasaur appear in the middle of the room and slowly twist and turn - a bit like a moment from the *Exorcist*. While creepy, I was surprised how easy the process was, and can see how creating more sophisticated experiences can be straightforward. It was also fantastic fun to use. The same goes for learning Spark AR; after a short evening, I made a face filter where it selects a random sports team. That ease meant that many AR creators could hop in and get their hands dirty. And for that reason, more and more people are having a go.

One exploding area is the use of face filters. In 2019 and early 2020, users witnessed a deluge of face filters in all sorts of styles. Some cycled through 'which Simpsons character are you', while others were trippy experiences that littered heads with eyes and mouths. Like a germ the filters spread quickly, as each user shared their result with hundreds or thousands of their followers. The network effect takes hold, and a filter could be seen millions of times - even tens of millions, in the case of some leading AR creators.

Albert Millis, COO of Virtual Umbrella, said 'AR filters from the very beginning had very low barriers of entry, meaning we had an avalanche of creativity from thousands of developers, artists and creators continually pushing what you can do with the face tracking technology. Now the bar is being raised every single day, and we are seeing some amazing stuff.'

One leading creative is Ommy Akhe. After following the Spark AR community group on Facebook,

Akhe wanted to have a go at making experiences herself. The result is some profound and beautiful experiences shared widely, which led to clients approaching her for her expertise.

Part of the growth is linked to the network appeal of Instagram. 'Instagram has such a unique and huge user base that people can't help but engage with filters,' Akhe told *The Verge* in 2019. 'I think being able to add filters to Stories has been a massive shift and change in Instagram culture.'[43]

Another great example is Liam O'Neill, a freelance AR creator with a stellar client list, including Adidas, North Face, Michael Kors, Amazon, Urban Outfitters, and many more. O'Neill receives client briefs and creates the filters for brands as part of their campaigns. His recent work with Adidas led to tens of millions of people seeing his work.

Gareth Leedling, Executive Creative Director at We Are Social, calls the current trend the face filter phenomenon. He is right. Few trends before have shown the breadth and depth of a face filter campaign, complemented with analytics to show its impact. O'Neill is a creative who has worked with the agency, and makes the experiences come to life.

As Instagram continues to grow in popularity (and Facebook dwindles), Stories are a great way to get a message out there. But it is also one example, not the sole

---

[43] Lee, Dami. "How Ommy Akhe Makes Her Ultra-Cool Instagram AR Filters." The Verge, 22 Nov. 2019,
https://www.theverge.com/2019/11/22/20963747/ommy-akhe-instagram-filters-spark-ar-augmented-reality.

one. AR is powerful beyond the big tech giants, which must be kept in mind as marketers follow the tech.

It is why I believe WebAR is a big deal. Not everyone uses the same applications globally; Instagram is prominent in Europe, but Snapchat is more significant in the US. While texting is still the go-to means of communicating in many US states, India uses WhatsApp. Not all platforms are equal in all countries. But absolutely everyone has a mobile device and access to a web browser. That ease of access cannot be underestimated and has been used by several companies to significant effect.

The first step to decide is the platform. Brands can deliver their content via WebAR, Instagram, Snapchat, and many others. The first step is to get to the heart of the project, and pin down the best approach. For example, if a drinks company wants to maximise its packaging as a marketing channel, then WebAR would be the most suitable. If it is a branded campaign to target teenagers, then an Instagram face filter would be powerful as well.

Like all platforms, Instagram has some curation. The company banned filters relating to plastic surgery, to make sure harmful ideals do not spread far. Instagram is also cutting down on other dangerous forms of content like self-harming. Individual creatives navigate these issues cleanly, advising their clients on the right ways of using the platform.

Stuart Cupit, Creative Technology Officer at Solarflare Studio, believes we should shift away from base experiences as well. 'We should try to get away from the gimmick and go towards something useful. We have seen so many gimmicks over the last few years, and we want to move from that to gain more traction.'

Approval times have lengthened as well. In the early days, it took a few hours for a filter to be approved. Now it can take up to a month - something which budding brands need to keep in mind when planning their campaigns. Both agencies and freelancers have deep expertise needed to run successful campaigns. Like any campaign, it takes collaboration and tenacity for success.

Ultimately, AR will not go away as a marketing medium. It provides a powerful and smart way for people to communicate their messages, allowing people to engage with their work like nothing else. Alongside the trend, AR creators are learning new skills and having a go themselves.

At a recent meet-up in Digital Catapult, several creatives noted that the number of people developing AR experiences is surging rapidly. As tools become more comfortable to use, more people are jumping on with bright ideas and a can-do attitude. All the AR creators welcomed the rise in competition and the corresponding increase in quality. Similarly, Blend Media is opening a marketplace for companies to be connected to professionals so that people can be connected to new work.

Through the 2020s, more freelancers and agencies will be working with companies to market their brands in several new ways. While platforms may change, the heart stays the same: AR is an engaging and immersive way to interact with users and practical as well. It's a new and significant career-path to watch out for.

DRONES: ZOOMING IN FIRST PERSON

Virtual reality cameras are a great way to bring a person into an immersive experience. From something as small as a live stream of kittens to investigative reports in international conflicts, virtual reality drones bring content to a whole new level. Yet while creators make videos on the ground, recording from high in the sky takes the next step forward. Because of this, the best virtual reality drones balance between usability and durability, able to take a hit while flying safely.

Virtual reality drones are flying devices that have the capability of filming or streaming immersive content. The content is then viewable in a VR headset. The idea is that people can fly their drones around, have the material recorded, and then watchable later for professional or personal purposes.

That said, it is not viewable or filmable in 'true' virtual reality. Real VR is what you can expect to see in Oculus Rift S, Oculus Quest, or HTC Vive units. The footage is much more immersive, allowing people to explore a new virtual world. (A lidar unit or photogrammetry can be used to capture 3d space to make it more immersive). When people say virtual reality, what they mean is 360 video, where people can look around and see the world around them. It is less immersive but no less powerful.

As people mean 360 videos when they say virtual reality drones, the term will be used throughout this chapter for the sake of simplicity.

Drone racers use FPV goggles to improve their racing skill. By equipping the drones with a small camera, racers feel like they are piloting at the front of the device. It means they can take better turns around a course, without making mistakes by viewing the race from an outside perspective.

While the FPV goggles look like VR headsets, the truth is that they are not. They are rudimentary goggles that display a 2D view of the race, not a 360 experience that can be looked around left and right. Racers also do not need VR; they need to look ahead, making sure they do not crash.

Because of this, the chapter will not focus on racing drones or their FPV goggles; though they are still very, very stylish, as shown below. What this chapter will instead focus on is the best drones for filming immersive 360 content.

So let's start with the first kind, relating to filming drones. For this, I spoke to Ben Huss-Smickler, Head of Immersive at SkyEdge360. He is an expert who has been shooting with drones for years, to get his insights into the area.

There are two ways to film, and both come down to quality. Two lens cameras work on a smaller drone, which can fly in the air for longer. The drones are typically easier to transport, quicker to set up, and nimble enough to hover close to their subjects without harming the person or object. But the disadvantage is that the resolution is not as high, reaching 5.7K; high for video, but not good enough for 360 videos. The lenses also shoot at 30fps, when 60fps is preferable.

The second is using a larger drone for shots. These are bulky and difficult to carry and do not last in the air for as long. While stable, they cannot be near specific targets for filming. But the benefit is that they can carry powerful cameras that can provide the very best quality. An example is the Titan, which can shoot in 11K, more than what any headset in the market can handle. For quality, this is the one to use.

These two types are the norm for filmers around the world today. But in the future, there will be a new class which will make filming much more accessible.

Mr Huss-Smickler notes that an upcoming class of drone is more suitable for filming in virtual reality, called Ciniwhoop. These drones are small, about 250g to 500g, and can usually be 3D-printed for use. These smaller drones are similar to the kind which racers use, such as Promark, though build to carry cameras.

While other types of drones have been retrofitted to work with filming, this class has been designed from the ground-up to work with filming. It is also intended to be under 250g or 500g, which means it circumvents laws in some countries on declaring the drones which can be used for filming.

While this is a little into the future, keen enthusiasts can have a go with their own hands. For those who want to dip their toes into printing their drones, this resource page outlines everything you need to know on how to start. The page also describes some groups to access and raise questions, and where hobbyists can dip in to answer. Alternatively, the chapter will list a few drones which work for the hobbyists who want to dip their toes into the area.

These drones can also be used for photography, not just filming. Taking flight, users can don their FPV goggles and surf above some waves or crest mountains, snapping 360 shots to take back home. Once returned, they can then be used on Facebook to make 360 banners or photos, which can provide an all-encompassing view of a holiday or trip. While films can show more action, a photo taken at the right time can speak volumes.

The drones listed in this chapter have those same capabilities. Some drones, like the Promark, are good enough. Others, like the DJI Mavic Pro 2, are top in their class. But the best virtual reality drones can also shoot film, for those who want to show the environment in action.

It is one thing to own a drone; it is quite another to be allowed to fly it. With the spate of high-profile drone incidents around the world, countries have placed regulations to ensure that they cannot be flown unless certain conditions are set. These rules differ from country to country, even within the European Union.

The first step every person should take is to contact the country's Civil Aviation Authority. The aviation regulators provide advice and steps to take in order to gain permission in each country, and can guide people in the right direction.

From there, the flyer would typically need to get permission for aerial work, otherwise known as a PFAW. In the UK's case, flyers would need to take a theory test, write an operations manual, and take practical tests. Such tests are extensive and time-consuming, but are necessary to ensure the safety of areas being filmed. (PFAW is only necessary for commercial work, if it is recreational it is not necessary).

Once acquired, there are still restrictions on what a PFAW can allow. For example, certain locations – such as sites of historical interest – are banned unless an additional layer of permission is granted. Further, there is a general rule that a drone cannot be within 50 meters of a person or object outside of the crew's control. An aeronautical map can show where is restricted airspace. To gain access, flyers also need a NOTAM.

These rules are complicated and restrictive but are there to ensure that virtual reality drones do not overstep their boundaries. In any case, the best first case is to contact the Civil Aviation Authority and take the necessary steps.

The future will likely bring further iterations of virtual reality drones, while becoming more accessible for consumers with lower costs.

Currently, virtual reality drones are primarily dominated by hobbyists and professionals who use the capabilities for multiple activities, from filming films to racing around courses. Buying them is relatively easy, but using them well takes time and effort. Given time, drones will decrease in cost allowing more people to buy them, and resources are more accessible so more people can play with them.

Another potential innovation is the use of augmented reality (AR). By using the drones' internal GPS and trackers placed on the ground, racecourses could be overlaid via AR, with floating virtual targets to hit as drones fly around. While this is not directly related to virtual reality drones, the use of AR will impact the way drones could be controlled and used, improving the user experience.

ARCADES: THE GATEWAY TO VR

Virtual reality arcades offer an excellent experience for people first trying VR. Arcades let people play games while others can watch, trying out a new headset with friends and family. From parties to events, they are a lot of fun for everyone.

Several words describe virtual reality arcades. PubVR experiences are a personal favourite, though VRcade is an excellent, short-form way of describing it. But generally, the public recognises it as a way to play VR experiences without having an expensive headset. It is fun to immerse yourself in a new adventure. For this reason, and many others, arcades are going to be necessary for VR adoption.

There are various locations around the UK, particularly in London. IPG has several installations, including the Elephant Arena and the Four Thieves. Occasionally, the Loading Bar hosts VR setups as well. In Nottingham, Zero Latency opened a warehouse-scale installation, where people fight zombies in multiplayer games.

All these arcades have in common is that they can be used outside a home, among friends and family. It adds a social element to the virtual reality experience.

Since 2014, when Facebook bought Oculus, there has been a resurgence of companies making virtual reality games for players to use. The PSVR has seen great success with new IPs like Tetris Effect and ASTRO BOT. The Oculus Rift, alongside the Oculus Go, has seen some significant interest among technology journalists and enthusiasts alike. The HTC Vive is also a popular virtual reality headset, with very high fidelity and quality, while standalone headsets are getting more popular.

Some party games work very well in the home. *Beat Saber*, a personal favourite, gets people in the mood and swinging to play games. *Beat Saber* is also great for cardio, something which many players may not have the time to do otherwise.

In virtual reality arcades, set-ups usually have the HTC Vive. With its reliability and quality of controls, the virtual reality headset provides many experiences for players to use and play with. Provided that there are clean tissues to wipe the sweaty lenses afterwards, the games are set.

Here, Sam Watts again has some extensive thoughts on the topic, after assisting for so many years:

'Back in 2014 I filmed a piece about the rise of VR arcades for Vice, which unfortunately got left on the digital cutting room floor, when talking about Oculus Rift DK1 and VR gaming adoption as part of the annual Develop: Brighton conference. However my words still ring true today, 6+ years later as VR gaming, according to some, is still struggling to gain the mainstream foothold that analysts predicted back at the start of the current resurgent wave of VR.

'VR headsets, and the hardware required to run them for PC VR have gotten cheaper, more capable and more appealing over the past few years, with room-scale and fully-tracked devices being the norm' now. As with all technology though, especially PCs, the average cost for the hardcore gamer always seems to stay around the same for the high-end; you just get more bang for your buck. With the advent of standalone devices, although not as graphically powerful as the PC VR tethered devices, the barriers to entry are dropping away along with the friction points that make getting into VR fussy and messy. However one thing hasn't changed - the space requirements to do full VR experiences; players houses haven't miraculously gotten bigger over time.

'This is where I predicted VR arcades would excel and create a resurgence in the out-of-home entertainment sector - the ability to do full VR at a scale intended to provide immersive experiences is just not possible at home. Whilst many 'mom & pop' arcades have appeared in towns and cities across the globe, offering access to VR hardware and experiences that you could get at home, many dedicated, bespoke custom setups are making waves in dedicated locations offering experiences that simply can not be done elsewhere.

'Both types of arcade serve valid purposes however certainly now and for the immediate foreseeable future - whilst the hardware gets cheaper, the cost is still prohibitive to many and as a dedicated device, a considerable investment to one purpose. So just being able to go some place and experience VR helps provide those initial touch points and interactions, increasing excitement and desire and helping some of those concerns or negative connotations, thanks to mostly negative traditional gaming press coverage around nausea every time VR is mentioned, fade away.

'Where location-based-entertainment VR (LBEVR) really excels is providing those large scale, free-roaming, multi-user experiences that are unique to the design and options offered by having vastly larger play spaces, that become a complete out-of-home unique offering and group outing option beyond other traditional entertainment venues. With additional elements adding further dimensional inputs, like temperature, motion, haptics and networked avatar representation, venue customers can really feel like they are experiencing something out of this world that isn't possible anywhere else in their current lifetime.

'But the initial resurgence of VR was plagued by a blinkered over-emphasis on the possibilities of new forms of gaming, many of which are still to come to light or be presented in a polished manner, limiting the interest and appeal of the new devices to a hardcore, enthusiast audience only. What many locations and venues are realising now is that VR can be used for so much more than just gaming and shooting things in the face, and so dedicated 360º film cinemas, immersive theatres, relaxation centers, interactive art and museum installations are appearing in existing and new venues alike to widen audience attentions and interests.

'We are still at a stage where the majority count out of 10 haven't tried VR before. Those that have will often state they didn't like it or it made them feel sick. They will typically confirm this was with a low-end VR headset running off a mobile phone, usually running a simple rollercoaster experience. Something about VR inhibits considerations of the wider potential amongst first-time users, creating an internal binary decision; they either did or didn't like that particular experience and that defines whether they are willing to try another one, without realising that it's a new medium, and just like the Google Cardboard, just because you don't like a particular TV show doesn't mean you can dismiss the entire programme guide forever more.

'What location based venues have to do is ensure they have the best intentions at heart for VR and ensure that each person who enters their premises leaves with a positive outlook on the technology and what it's capable of - ideally excited enough to go to the shops and purchase a headset for themselves.'

Again, I thank Sam for his contributions.

The cost of running a VR arcade is expensive. The first step is to rent space, which is extortionate in London. Combined with expensive PCs that need to be consistently maintained alongside expensive headsets, and you have an expensive down-cost to start out. Then there needs to be a trained attendant who handles the virtual reality headsets, making sure they do not break. Drunk people may play, which adds a layer of risk.

If the VR arcade gets a flow of customers who use the set-up, then it may work well for the company. Arcades have already seen enough success to appear in the UK and USA, and continued growth is expected.

All that being said, here is where virtual reality arcades flourish. In the case of *Serious Sam*, players can shoot zombies together, much like co-op play with *Call of Duty* many years ago. Among colleagues, it is a great team bonding exercise as well. Companies encourage colleagues to leave the office and have a pint, to de-stress and bond over non-work matters. In the same way, having a VR experience with colleagues is an excellent use of finances and time. The experiences do not necessarily have to be bloody or violent, as there are escape room experiences as well.

In any case, immerse yourself into a new experience and have fun. Yet sometimes, they can fold.

Case Study: IMAX VR

IMAX made some hefty investments into VR a few years ago, making a variety of IMAX VR centers in the US. It was a pilot program, an exploration of something new. It also had $50 million in VC funding, a substantial amount. The VR centre initially opened in New York, L.A., Manchester, Bangkok, Shanghai, and Toronto.

However, in late 2018 the company announced that it would be closing down its centers, with no further investment through 2019. A spokesperson said they would conclude the program by the end of Q1 2019.

In short, the virtual reality arcades closed down due to lack of interest after substantial funding. The experiment failed, and it may indicate a general slow-down in the market. IMAX virtual reality now rests in the history books.

Yet despite the potential lack of interest, there are plenty of great games out there to try out with friends.

Reports indicate that interest is steadily growing. Greenlight Insights report that arcades provide consumers with a way to demo VR. It provides a cheap, easy way to try it out without a powerful PC or headset. It means customers are interested in trying them out and buying a set for themselves. According to a survey, 53 per cent of consumers are interested in arcades.[44]

It may change in the future as headsets enter the home. With a premium experience ready to be played with, then people may be less likely to go back to arcades. However, this is far in the future, and for now, arcades provide a gateway to great games to play.

Cleaning the headset afterwards is incredibly essential. Germs can spread very quickly, and no user wants to have a hot and misty headset after vigorous use. Wet wipes should be used liberally.

Seeing a great business opportunity, many companies are investigating arcades for play. Popping up all over the place, the immersive experiences are capitalising on a new experience for those who want to play.

In the past, some immersive experiences folded; partially due to the high costs of setting up and running the place, partly because the audience lost interest. If a VR company attempts to make more virtual reality arcades, they must provide a value proposition which will continually bring new people to the place. Then, the arcade will thrive.

With the new wave of immersive reality, time will tell whether they will stick. For now, there is always a

---

[44] "VR Arcades Are Hot Trend, But Consumers Want So Much More." Greenlight Insights, 24 Feb. 2018, https://greenlightinsights.com/vr-arcades-consumers-want-more-location-based-vr/.

subtle draw to the arcade cabinet – more so if a headset is rigged to it.

Case Study – Zero Latency

Zero Latency invited Virtual Perceptions to try out their warehouse-scale VR experience in Boxpark Wembley, London. We tried co-op zombie shooting, co-op sci-fi adventuring, and competitive PVP shooting during our press day.

Our experiences were incredibly positive. Zero Latency shows that VR has a place for parties and events, where the technology is excellent fun for anyone to use. The experience sits alongside laser tag and go-karting as fun for large groups of friends.

Before we headed into the game, the staff gave us a short rundown of what to expect. This included health and safety, how to wear the PC backpack, and how to not hit each other in the face.

A great feature is the proximity alarm. When players are too near one another, an alert flashes on the screen for how close the person is. It means it is more difficult to hit one another whilst in combat.

We were presented with guns, a Microsoft headset, an HP backpack, and a microphone. Decked together, we walked into the room.

The first experience is a zombie survival game. The six of us are army officers, debris flaming around us. The goal is to survive as long as possible while racking up the points, as the horde clambers to our location.

Each of the physical guns has a button, where the weapons can be flipped from one to another, such as an assault rifle or a shotgun. Marking ourselves around the map, we held them back with spurts of gunfire.

The game is similar to the zombie mode in Call of Duty, where players guard a house and hold off against increasingly powerful foes. What's amusing is that players can walk onto a lift to go up some scaffolding, which plays tricks on the mind as the players are actually in the same location.

The game generously gives points to headshots, hugely rewarding accuracy over-spraying bullets. But in the end, the points didn't matter; it was the survival against the odds until we were lifted into the sky and Gatling guns blazed and lit the sky.

The headset was not loud enough to pick up one another's voices; short snippets of help were drowned by the snarls and blasts of the night air. While being distinctly aware, we were in a Zero Latency warehouse.

But the camaraderie of working together is excellent fun. Wandering around the warehouse to defeat the foes was a great way to bond together, particularly with players whom I had not met before.

The next one is more of a story. A team of soldiers with pulsating laser guns wander through a spaceship, teaming together to fight robots that act like zombies (as opposed to zombie robots).

The game is very similar to zombie survival with the types of guns available, only this time players progress from room to room, shooting enemies as they appear or navigating tight ledges.

The game gave me an Aliens vibe, where people wander around a spaceship trying not to be killed by creatures around the corner.

The challenge came at the end, with a major boss battle against what can only be described as Metal Gear. We kept dying as missiles blasted us, so we adapted by focusing fire on the drones and body parts.

Singularity was great. By the end, we felt like soldiers lifting the mask to grey reality. We were also very, very sweaty in the Zero Latency arena.

The final experience was exceptional. It is the worlds first PVP esports experience, designed for an audience. It was necessary to capture the flag experience, where players roam around a map and shoot one another.

While initially slow, the pace picked up as we got used to the gameplay. Some of us were more aggressive, some more methodical. But in any case, it felt great to pop some heads.

The merits of the experience as an esport is worthy of further debate. But in the case of just fun with friends, it is great to play in for the moment.

Overall, Zero Latency offers an excellent experience for players who want a fun bash with friends over the weekend or in the evenings. Taken together, all the VR games give players a wealth of choice on what to do. Zero Latency is the seminal example of a successful VR arcade.

MEDITATION: QUIET IN A LOUD WORLD

Stress cripples modern society. Not in the visible, limping way of a dislocated leg, or a broken arm. Stress paralyzes the mind, a thousand anxious thoughts processing at once. Many people use guided meditation apps to help ease their anxieties. Meditation in VR takes it to another level – with great benefits for the user. There are VR meditation videos on YouTube, or guided meditation apps on VR headsets. What works? What are the benefits of VR meditation? And how is it different from normal meditation?

Meditation in VR is the use of headsets to focus the mind and reach a mentally calm state of being. The process is similar to the usual meditation techniques. The user sits down, enters a tranquil state of mind, and follows their breathing in and out. The aim is to focus on the breath without changing its pace or intensity; if the mind takes a walk, pull it back on the breath. It improves concentration while easing the brain of stress. Scientists widely report health benefits.[45] It means eyes are usually closed, creating a panel of darkness which acts like a tapestry where thoughts can float across. There are no external inputs, nor shifting pictures. With meditation in VR, the user is surrounded by an environment which contributes to the experience.

Cubicle Ninjas made *Guided Meditation VR*, a popular VR app. The app is diverse with 22 environments

---

[45] Todd, Carolyn L. "Here's What Meditation Can—and Can't—Do for Your Health." SELF, https://www.self.com/story/mindfulness-meditation-health-benefits. Accessed 18 Feb. 2020.

to sit and meditate in, like the moon, or other spots to rest under the stars. The content can be customised, drawing from experts to create relaxing experiences for the user. I used the app, and it placed me on the moon. It was peaceful, calming, and overall very fun. I sat there for a long time, absorbed by the setting, and felt my mind calming with time. When I took my Oculus off, the world was quiet. It is a great way to start with guided meditation in VR, and it is available on all major platforms (HTC Vive, Oculus Rift, Oculus Go, Gear VR).

This topic means a lot to me personally as I work in London. Work can be fast, and overwhelming, and meditation grants context to the chaos. The modern life has two lives. One is the work-life, with a stream of chattering emails, meetings, and plans of increasing complexity and depth. Work is not just noise, but a thousand soft voices speaking simultaneously. It sucks energy from the second life, sapping energy until the home life is a person curled on the sofa watching Russel Howard on a Friday evening. VR mindfulness can help with this, giving context and assisting people to deal with the stress of everyday life. A calm outlook can solve the principle issue of modern city life. After my positive experience, I highly recommend donning the headset and having a go.

ETHICS IN VIRTUAL AND AUGMENTED REALITY

Like veins in rocks, ethics runs through everything we do in technology. It depends on how we use it, but it can still be used for evil as much as good. Sometimes it is a hard impact. Facebook allows microtargeting which could radicalise people, spurring them towards violence and terrorism. Or it is softer, like Instagram giving a generation of young people image problems as they compare themselves to unattainable standards. A fundamental ethical framework on how we use tools can save and improve lives. The same goes for immersive technologies like AR and VR, where communicating in virtual worlds could have drastic effects on people and societies.

Take mobile phones. Just a few decades ago, people planned to meet friends, relying on being prompt without ways to communicate. Then friends invest time in each other without distractions, with a lot of meaning as it was rarer to speak. And news came mainly from the well-funded print houses of Fleet Street, with the personnel and time to pursue investigative news stories to inform their readers.

That has changed. Friends became laxer with timings, flinging a message if they are late. Once together, friends stick to their phones in fear of missing something important. And journalism? Struggling, as online platforms enabled a deluge of free ways to read the news of varying quality, hitting larger companies hard who can't pursue the projects they want.

None of this is necessarily bad. It is beautiful to connect with friends thousands of miles away or be able to access the world's knowledge in your hand (if you can read through the torrent of noise). But these changes happened, and their impact changed the way we communicate around the world. Predicting these changes, and planning accordingly, is essential.

Many people think this is underexplored, a desert of information compared to the bounty of experiences already available on platforms. In reality, a fair few professors stepped forward to investigate ethics in immersive media. Their conclusions could reveal a very different society in the future, changed as much as when the mobile phone entered the mainstream.

Environment shapes people. Place one person in a war-torn country, and another in a luxury lifestyle. Both will have different views of what is right and wrong, formed by their experiences.

The same goes for virtual reality. Companies create new environments to train workers the right process relevant to their job roles. Immerse, a UK-based enterprise company, helped recreate an entire submarine, to guide employees around the sophisticated machinery of the machine. Submersing them in the environment helps them helps to embed the learning in their minds, far better than reading from a manual or an instructor who has to describe the surroundings.

People can use technology for good too. VR can be an empathy machine, bringing people together and informing them of new concepts and, eventually, converting them. In one study, it helps to identify with different people around the world.[46]

---

[46] Nakamura, Lisa. "Virtual Reality and the Feeling of Virtue: Women of Color Narrators, Enforced Hospitality, and the Leveraging of Empathy." Proceedings of the 2019 on Designing Interactive Systems Conference - DIS '19, ACM Press, 2019, pp. 3–3. DOI.org (Crossref),

But these simulated environments can harm users too. Erick Jose Ramirez notes that virtual spaces let neuroscience researchers look beyond the ethical issues of placing people in real-life hazardous areas. While they cannot put them in dangerous places (psychologically speaking), why not a virtual one instead? Surely it bypasses any health issues?[47]

Ramirez disagrees, and it deserves greater scrutiny. These virtual environments can hurt people as much as the real experiment, only not as well regulated.

Ramirez cited the Milgram Shock Experiment to support his point. For those unfamiliar, it tests the obedience of people to follow orders despite hearing the pain of others. Every time they are told to press the button, they hear a scream of pain. They are asked to touch it again, and again, and again, to see how far they would go. The purpose was to see how long people would follow orders that inflict harm, related to the atrocities inflicted by service people during World War Two.

In a later paper, Mel Slater argued that a simulated environment would have the same negative ramifications on the user psychologically, even if they performed in a virtual space.[48] Though the participants are fake, the users learn that they are capable of harm; an ethical issue raised regardless of the realism of the experiment.

---

doi:10.1145/3322276.3325420.
[47] Ramirez, Erick Jose. "Ecological and Ethical Issues in Virtual Reality Research: A Call for Increased Scrutiny." Philosophical Psychology, vol. 32, no. 2, Feb. 2019, pp. 211–33. Taylor and Francis+NEJM, doi:10.1080/09515089.2018.1532073.
[48] Slater, Mel, et al. "A Virtual Reprise of the Stanley Milgram Obedience Experiments." PLoS ONE, edited by Aldo Rustichini, vol. 1, no. 1, Dec. 2006, p. e39. DOI.org (Crossref), doi:10.1371/journal.pone.0000039.

With the increased realism of today's VR, Ramirez argues that VR needs more regulation for experiments. Like a loophole in a legal battle, people could use the technology to run tests which harm users, regardless of their realism.

Currently, no such guidelines exist. So Ramirez proposed The Equivalence Principle: 'If it would be wrong to subject a person... then it would be wrong to subject a person to a virtually-real analog of that experience. As a simulation's likelihood of inducing virtually-real experiences in its subject increases, so too should the justification for the experimental protocol.'

Ramirez is right to call out that VR should not be used to bypass specific laws and ethics of experimentation. Over the next decade, we may see more and more use cases of VR putting users under undue stress, which could compromise their psychology and hurt them. Bodies should put simulations under greater scrutiny.

These same concerns arise in journalism, as companies explore using VR for their reporting.[49] Journalism raises the same issues; if we misuse VR, then it could harm groups as it is so powerful and immersive. The consensus was that journalists should uphold the same Press Ethics guidelines they already use in print. A small but necessary step to ensure the high quality of journalism.

The hope is that, as VR becomes more ubiquitous, there will be more demand for 360 storytelling. When that happens, reporters can deliver compelling stories, similar to what the New York Times and the Guardian are currently doing.

---

[49] Sánchez Laws, Ana Luisa, and Tormod Utne. "Ethics Guidelines for Immersive Journalism." Frontiers in Robotics and AI, vol. 6, 2019. Frontiers, doi:10.3389/frobt.2019.00028.

The overall theme of both experimentation and journalism is reporters should follow the rules and provide compelling stories. The trouble is, it can be used to abuse as well.

One last area I want to explore is the social implications of AR glasses. Through the 2020s we should expect to see AR glasses to enter, and probably rupture, the market. As they become a fashion accessory, more and more people will be wearing glasses and communicating with one another.

What is unknown is the changes in socialising that would occur, similar to how the ubiquity of mobile phones changed us over the last few decades.

In theory, it would not change much. Instead of glancing under the table, people could look forwards and scan their messages on their lenses, scrolling with simple inputs with the mind. Less antisocial than looking away from a friend mid-conversation, though the brain would be focusing on other matters regardless.

But one potential issue is being always connected to the virtual world. Mobile phones can be restricted by turning them off and putting them in your pocket and disconnect. The mobile phone is separate from the person. For many, the detox is bliss. But glasses-wearers are reliant on them to see, so they would continuously be, quite literally, on their face. How can people cope with constant connectivity, as their real and virtual world merges for all hours of their day? How would that change a person and their grip on reality?

Violent actions in VR or AR is also worthy of exploration as well. Researchers have confirmed that there is not a link between video game violence and real-life violence. But will VR have a greater impact, by placing people in virtual environments to kill? Tom Pascoe, an AR developer, agrees that this is important to follow as well, highlighting the surge of violent YouTube videos where people enjoy killing online.

Then there is the security of data, according to Damien Mason at ProPrivacy. Damien gives his thoughts:

'Cameras and even microphones are used throughout both technologies, helping virtual reality headsets to gauge distance and allowing augmented reality programs to superimpose digital objects into the real world.

'Offline, this might not be a problem. But since users are almost always connected to the internet, it's questionable just how much of this data is being collected by respective companies.

'Since companies realise that the average person doesn't read terms and conditions, the right to collect the location you live in, the things you say to other players, the food you eat and many more bits of information you wouldn't begin to consider is usually buried deep within privacy policies, but it's a genuine possibility. European law such as the General Data Protection Regulation has tried to curb shady practices within the region and there are respectable developers that only collect the data necessary to run their software, but it's always worth keeping an eye out for the majority that still takes whatever they can get.'

Based on these arguments, we should focus on the following principles for ethics in VR and AR. These are deliberately open-ended, to develop as we develop the technology further:

1) **Hold virtual spaces to the same standards as real ones.** Both journalists and neuroscientists agree that the same rules of real-life should apply to VR. VR

has the power to change, influence, or hurt participants if misused, and should be regulated to guidelines as much as possible. While VR can change people, such as with empathy, its capacity for harm is apparent.

2) **Differentiate between thrill and harm.** Horror VR games can give us a thrill, as they force us to confront fears. But a line should be drawn between horror and deliberate harm; a path that is difficult to draw but is still present.

3) **Be aware of how social interaction will change as AR glasses arrive.** While not necessarily bad, the arrival of AR glasses will likely change how we socialise with one another in the same way that mobile phones have. We are beginning to understand how mobile phones have changed us today; how will glasses do the same in a few decades?

CONTROL: REGULATION AND RISKS IN THE FUTURE

Immersive technologies will revolutionise the future. From movies and arcades to healthcare and manufacturing, immersive technologies will impact every area of society and work. Current cost restrictions will likely pass with time, pick-up will likely increase, and adoption will become widespread. The technology will set itself into society, another tool to complement the array available to consumers and workers; valuable, indispensable, and widely used.

Then the next danger comes in.

Any technology that embeds into society inevitably evolves its people. When mobile phones were adopted several years ago, concurrent studies have shown that many people have shorter attention spans when consuming content.[50] Equipped with mini-computers that can tap into the entire known knowledge of humankind, or social media networks that hook people with dopamine loops, and the way people interact irreparably changed. Instead of planning meetups to catch up with friends and family, groups can coordinate online. People are influenced by online personalities, as influencers on YouTube or Twitter could hold more sway for some people than traditional newspapers. Entertainment moved from analogue TVs with set schedules towards streaming services where plans are

---

[50] Wright, Mike, and Ellie Zolfagharifard. "Internet Is Giving Us Shorter Attention Spans and Worse Memories, Major Study Suggests." The Telegraph, 6 June 2019. www.telegraph.co.uk, https://www.telegraph.co.uk/technology/2019/06/06/internet-giving-us-shorter-attention-spans-worse-memories-major/.

irrelevant, and binging is accepted. These changes are so pervasive, so set into society, that the above observations seem obvious. But what is most remarkable of all is that they only occurred within the last thirty years, a speck of time in the history of humanity.

The same will happen with immersive technology. In every part of society, people will change alongside the tools they use. As they envelop themselves in new equipment, a new kind of interaction could evolve with time. Changes in the way people interact tend to change the rules of social interaction, adding a new layer in which people converse with one another.

And with the dangers that come forward, it is critical to regulating technology before it becomes an issue.

Let's take Facebook as an example. Facebook's experiment with a brain-reading interface was inevitable. As the company continues to develop their AR glasses, the input method is one of the most important qualities as it must be as accessible and straightforward as possible. No-one wants to fiddle with buttons or external controllers; the most frictionless way to swipe through an AR lens is the mind itself. The final stage for a completely seamless experience is not using any fingers at all.

However, that would mean Facebook needs to read the mind. This is dangerous without proper regulation. Following Cambridge Analytica, Facebook has shown that they treat data as an asset, and the company can exploit it for more value. Facebook already has enough information to understand every human on its network, more profound than the people themselves. If the company also had access to the brain, then the complexity and richness of the data available could be dangerous for one company to handle.

It is critical to explore now. Regulators are notoriously slow to react to upcoming developments, so they should be acting now before Facebook makes significant steps in the technology. Also, AR glasses are set to become the next global hardware trend; with billions of people affected by poor eyesight, Facebook (and Apple) are primed to dominate a market with their products. The time to act is now.

On July 30 2019, Facebook published a blog post with an update on its brain-reading computer interface. Organised by University of California researchers backed by Facebook Reality Labs, the company detailed the results of an experiment in decoding words via implanted electrodes. University subjects listened to multiple-choice questions and answered them aloud; then electrodes recorded the corresponding activity in the brain. The team looked for the patterns that corresponded with the exact words, linking the two together. From this procedure, the system can associate brain patterns with names.[51]

It was not an extensive experiment. It was tightly controlled, with only nine questions and 24 possible answers. The implants were highly invasive, closely connected to the brain. Moreover, the patients were reciting the answers out loud, rather than just thinking them. If the researchers were developing a car, they have only managed to make a metal frame, devoid of wheels or components. In

---

[51] Imagining a New Interface: Hands-Free Communication without Saying a Word. https://tech.fb.com/imagining-a-new-interface-hands-free-communication-without-saying-a-word/. Accessed 24 Feb. 2020.

its current form, it is a far cry from the science fiction future of conducting applications with thoughts alone.

Yet even in its primitive state, it gives a glimpse into the future. As Facebook says in its post, 'being able to decode even just a handful of imagined words — like 'select' or 'delete' — would provide entirely new ways of interacting with today's VR systems and tomorrow's AR glasses.' Beyond this, the mind can compose a text message, then send it to their friends, without using hands.

Reading the brain is one red flag. The system would allow users to 'type' sentences out relatively quickly, with the system soon interpreting the brain's signals into readable content. Once sent, that data would then be on the network. Encrypted, but still stored.

The other red flag – no, the ten red flags billowing on top of a warning sign starring a red flag – is how Facebook analyses the data. The company can extrapolate the intentions, personality, and interests of a person based on what is said, profiling the user. A conversation is worth more than its words; it can be broken down and expanded to create hundreds of different conclusions about a person.

Now imagine the kind of sensitive data Facebook can pull directly from the mind. When someone types a text, we are presenting a curated version of ourselves, which we then send to our friends or family. We articulate the words, then send over the internet. However, imagine if Facebook could read the mind without the articulation stage; raw, transparent thoughts with no filter, without being translated to a screen. Currently, Facebook reads all our posts; the next step is understanding how posts are read and interpreted by users.

Facebook's likely counter-argument is that the user's data will be private. Since F8 earlier this year, the company made clear that they are designing privacy into the core of every product. All of Facebook's messenger apps will have end-to-end encryption. Also, an independent board will oversee Facebook's actions.

Problem solved, right? Facebook is pivoting the definition of privacy to rectify its public image, to become a company that can be trusted by its users. Except after a $5bn fine from the Federal Trade Commission, the largest in its history, Facebook's stock price rose. It was fine with little control over how the company runs itself. The action was a feeble, weak attempt to reign in the platform, a slap on the wrist rather than removing the limbs themselves.

Facebook retains some flexibility, meaning it can conduct further activities while ensuring the data is not shared with outside parties as easily. As Matt Levine points out, 'Facebook did some things that [many] people are upset about, some of which (certain sorts of data sharing) probably violated the laws or its earlier consent decrees, and others of which (certain sorts of data collection) didn't.' So the data is still being collected by the company – which can then be exploited by itself.

Brain activity goes beyond digital ethics towards a new area – neuroethics, the study of moral conduct relating to the mind. 'To me, the brain is the one safe place for freedom of thought, of fantasies, and for dissent,' Nita Farahany, a professor in neuroethics, told MIT Technology Review. 'We're getting close to crossing the final frontier of privacy in the absence of any protection whatsoever.'[52]

---

[52] Regalado, Antonio. "Facebook Is Funding Brain Experiments to

With a new level of intimacy, a new layer of rules should be introduced to protect users and their rights. Here are some suggested principles to follow:

- **Limited access.** Regulators should control which organisations can access and use the data; for example, political campaigns would have restricted access.
- **Transparent design.** The neuroethical design of Facebook's brain interface must be open and understandable by regulators and agencies, to fully understand what kind of data is collected.
- **Understandable algorithms**. Similarly, the way the data is used must be open and natural for regulators and agencies, to see how the information is interpreted and what new conclusions are drawn.
- **Ownership**. The user owns the data, not Facebook. If the user wishes for the data to be deleted, all data must be removed.
- **Open for users**. Any user can access the data Facebook has collected about themselves, and the types of conclusions the company has made from said data.
- **Active opt-in**. For every new update, Facebook outlines the details in a clear and concise way, and users opt into the ways in which their data will be used. This is so Facebook does not roll out a new

---

Create a Device That Reads Your Mind." MIT Technology Review, https://www.technologyreview.com/s/614034/facebook-is-funding-brain-experiments-to-create-a-device-that-reads-your-mind/. Accessed 24 Feb. 2020.

update with new capabilities that users passively accept; users actively need to understand what the new update is, and accept the impact it will have on their owned data.

The first three principles revolve around the design of the product. Facebook does not grant access to its algorithm easily nor explain how its algorithm works. That is understandable, as it is one of the most valuable formulas in the world. But regulators should understand how the data is processed and used. Then, the data's use is controlled to ensure that it leads to no harm or exploitation.

The last three revolve around the user. Data privacy revolves around ownership and use, and the user themselves should own the users' brain data. Facebook can use the information, but the user has much more control over how. The action ensures that the user fully consents to its use, as well as understanding how the company uses the information.

These principles are broad, encompassing the spirit of protecting users. Regulators should protect people from their data being used against them for nefarious purposes, and current legislation is inadequate for brain interfaces.

Then we should consider permissions as well. If no-one owns the virtual layer of reality, then anyone can abuse the space for their own gain. For example, McDonald's can put up virtual ads in all Burger Kings in the country. Dominic Collins, CEO of Darabase, has his own thoughts on the matter:

'As the immersive medium evolves, standard practices and regulations will undoubtedly apply. The consents and ways of working for all other media, for example Out of Home or copyrights and trademarks must apply to how commercial Augmented Reality content and advertising is displayed in physical locations.

'The vast majority of applications today are monetised through advertising and I'm sure immersive apps and layers will be no different. As an industry we need to create a way of serving branded and commercial content contextually into the GeoAR experience. It needs to be seamlessly served as though in the real world and not interruptive, as much of mobile inventory is today.

'AR advertising is already a billion dollar industry, but we're scratching the surface. The big opportunity comes as we move away from putting a lens on your face to augmenting the world around us. At Darabase we call this GeoAR - the potential is huge.

'If and when AR glasses start to replace our mobiles, an ever greater percentage of our digital lives will be displayed over and on the physical world. Not all of this will be persistent or specific to a particular location, but where it is property owners will have a significant incremental opportunity to control and monetise this new digital canvas. Darabase exists to facilitate this emerging ecosystem.'

Regulatory bodies are notoriously slow at responding to technology. Uber dominated the taxi industry before new city rules held them back. Airbnb's dominance closed hotels and impacted local communities before governments stepped in. Facebook's mishandling of people's data let campaign groups take dark approaches to win their political seats. Steps should be taken now to protect users in the future.

The clock is ticking.

EPILOGUE: WHERE IMMERSIVE TECHNOLOGY WILL GO NEXT

In 2019, standalone headsets like the Oculus Quest took the spotlight, selling units as fast as Facebook can make them. VR headsets for the PC were released as well, such as the Oculus Rift S, the Vive Cosmos, and the Valve Index, each with their perks and issues. All the while the PlayStation VR stayed strong, with rumours of a PSVR 2 coming soon. Immersive tech in 2020 will likely continue the battle for dominance in a rapidly competitive market.

The potential for growth is still there as companies continue to develop engagement technologies. Katherine Pearson, 5GRIT Alston Explorer and Time Traveler Maker, Flo-culture Ltd, believes that organisations in the visitor experience and tourism sector are eager to use new engagement technologies, as they are naturally progressing from their current activities.

Exciting times lie ahead as well. Facebook announced several upgrades for its Oculus Quest which could shape the future of VR, capitalising on the early success of its standalone headset. So what can we expect next year?

Compared to 2019, 2020 will likely be comparatively quiet. Facebook, HTC, and Valve all released new headsets, and it is unlikely that another headset in the same category would be released so soon. The same goes for VRgineers, whose XTAL headset still blows the specs of competitors out of the water.

But upgrades are more likely. For example, Facebook announced that hand tracking would be coming to the Oculus Quest in 2020. The feature would use the internal tracking already built into the headset, as an update to the released model. Facebook also announced Oculus Link, a way to connect the Oculus Quest to the PC so it can play Rift experiences. The development is a massive innovation that will shape the future of VR in 2020 and beyond.

Hardware manufacturers can also release a new headset in a different category. While HTC released the Vive Cosmos in 2019 for the PC platform, the standalone Vive Focus might be ready for an upgrade. As the Vive Focus is the portable and less powerful equivalent of the Vive Cosmos, the company may consider updating the hardware without cannibalising the PC market. HTC might also slash the costs as well, to compete with the Oculus Quest.

The exception is that the PlayStation VR is due an upgrade. Rumours about the PSVR 2 have circulated for several years, as Sony would like to follow up on the success of the original headset. 4.2 million headsets sold since launch is exceptional. The company may release the new hardware to coincide with its launch of the PlayStation 5.[53]

The immersive market will likely steadily improve. The first indication of a hockey-stick growth curve in 2019 was the launch of the Oculus Quest, and the subsequent rise in video game sales. But a steep improvement is not expected unless a new video game helps move hardware.

In any case, it is still an issue when not as many people can access the content. Take SideQuest, the third-party store for VR titles. The Oculus Quest store is a walled garden. Inside, great titles thrive under perfect conditions, with consistent promotions and the support of Facebook-

---

[53] Hamilton, Ian. "Sony Sold 4.2 Million PSVR Headsets." UploadVR, 25 Mar. 2019, https://uploadvr.com/sony-4-point-2-million-sold/.

owned Oculus. But their entry criteria are exact; not every software title can enter, vetted by employees monitoring for quality. Because of these restrictions, SideQuest's platform grew as anyone could submit content.

The Oculus Store serves casual browsers; people with a VR headset who purchase games on their established storefront. SideQuest is for more hardcore people who have the know-how to ready their Quest. While smaller, it is still a sizable amount.

The existence of SideQuest raises a few questions. On the one hand, we have a popular third-party platform where Oculus Quest games are sold. SideQuest doesn't get a cut of the game sales, but ads and Patreon run the platform itself. On the other, we have a goliath tech company who wants to run a curated apps platform, not open like Steam. Would there be conflict?

Initially, people may suspect that Oculus wants to close its competition. Having a store they 100 per cent control makes business sense. Not so; Oculus does not have those intentions. 'I have a great relationship with Oculus, we chat regularly, and it has always been positive,' said Shane Harris, CEO of SideQuest.

Instead, the relationship points towards SideQuest providing an alternative to the Oculus Quest store. 'The long term plan for SideQuest is to continue to deliver a useful facility for developers and users to enjoy. SideQuest has become a runaway success, so we are focused on managing that growth going forward.'

The strategy makes sense. Oculus monopolises the market by providing a store everyone has to use for purchases and discovery. The plan has worked wonders for Oculus, who reaped $100 million in software sales – 20 per cent of which from Quest titles sold in the four months before the announcement.[54]

By comparison, SideQuest has a slightly more complicated system where users need to make a developer account to sideload apps. Not easy for casual players who want to hop in and play. But despite this, SideQuest has 200,000 active users and 4,500,000 overall hits each month — a success by anyone's standards.

According to Mr Harris, FPS games are top-rated, such as *Pavlov, Crisis Vrigade*, and *Tea For God*. And developers are passionate about the platform too. Brett Jackson, the developer of *Jumbli*, notes that 'it provides an important place for experimentation and feedback for projects at an alpha/beta stage (replacing the long-gone Oculus Share) as well as generating revenue for VR developers.'

It is a make-or-break situation for Mr Jackson. 'The majority of my sales come from SideQuest, and without it, I may not have released the Quest version at all.

Mr Harris notes that the platform is consistently popular as its one of the few ways people can stream SteamVR to their Oculus Quest. He also remarks that there has been a rise in hand-tracking experiences; something that may further develop in the future.

In my view, the future seems right. With a positive relationship fulfilling two interested groups – casual browsers and hardcore enthusiasts – I can see both communities continuing to develop. Mr Harris provides an option for enthusiasts, while Oculus wants to have a

---

[54] McAloon, Alissa. 20% of the Oculus Store's $100 Million Lifetime Sales Were Quest Titles.
/view/news/351136/20_of_the_Oculus_Stores_100_million_lifetime_sales_were_Quest_titles.php. Accessed 24 Feb. 2020.

curated storefront, solving both wishes. And it is unlikely that Mr Harris currently cuts into the sales of the store, as its an additional ad-on for a different market.

Mr Jackson is positive about SideQuest. 'I'm grateful that Shane created SideQuest to give developers a way to reach the Quest players and share our efforts.'

At times, it is also notoriously difficult to keep track of stats on the immersive market. Superdata and CCS Insight keep track of the market, sometimes looking at both VR and AR together or overestimating the potential of some headsets. But collectively, all agree that the industry will develop steadily over the short-term.

Other technologies already help development. Burkhard Boeckem, CTO of Hexagon Geosystems, says that laser scanning technology and 3D mapping is already taking the industry by another level: 'As projects and scenes become more complex, and the need for accurate and instant data increases, new lightweight and mobile devices such as the Leica BLK2GO will allow teams to work faster and more efficiently... In the film industry, Industrial Light & Magic, the motion picture VFX company that's worked on films like Jurassic Park and Star Wars, also used 3D laser scanning for location scouting.'

Three trends and advancements will influence VR in 2020. The first is control methods and how people interact with experiences. The second is the merging of PC and standalone experiences into one system. The final one is around data privacy.

- **Control methods**. The way users interact in virtual reality must be designed to preserve or improve immersion. Controllers can be intuitive, but barriers can be broken down further to make the player feel more comfortable. Similarly, the Valve Index and its knuckle controllers are more intuitive than holding a typical games controller. In 2020, companies will likely announce new control methods.

- **Merging PC and standalone headsets.** Currently, the market is firmly divided between the two sides. On the one hand, PC headsets cannot be transported as easily but play powerful experiences. On the other, standalone experiences can be easily picked up, though with less graphical fidelity. But why not give VR headsets the functionality to do both? Why not have a standalone headset that can run its own experiences, but can also connect to a PC to play more graphically-intense adventures? The merge would collapse VR headsets into one, simplifying consumer choice. Also, Facebook has hinted at this with the Oculus Link, where the Oculus Quest can play Rift games.
- **Data privacy.** Consumers will raise questions around the privacy of user data with VR headsets. Damien Mason, a data privacy expert from ProPrivacy, says that 'VR headsets can collect audiovisual data of our surroundings and reserve the right to share these with third party companies within maddeningly vague guidelines.' He hopes to see concrete privacy policies emerge to outline what is collected. The approach would give users the right to opt-out, or enable greater punishments for those that misuse it.

Ultimately, the future rests on the content created by developers. The same virtuous cycle still applies; great VR games sells VR headsets, which in turn spurs more developers to make games for a bigger market. To achieve the goal, a few studios are focusing on either established IPs, or new experiences that use VR to its fullest.

Take *Medal of Honor: Above and Beyond*. Developed by Respawn Entertainment, the game uses the IP to make an experience designed for VR from the ground up. But there are two key reasons why gamers are interested in the game. The first is Respawn's pedigree, as the developers behind *Apex Legends* and *Titanfall*. But the second is equally important: *Medal of Honor* brand awareness. People are more likely to follow the game because it is connected to such an established video game franchise. Then people would be interested in the game and, hopefully, the exclusive platform it is on, the Oculus Rift S. The same goes for *Vader Immortal*, a Star Wars game that was designed exclusively for the Oculus Quest to shift more units.

Other developers are taking a different approach and creating unique experiences that then spreads via smart marketing and word of mouth. *Beat Saber* is the best example of this. The team developed a brand-new experience that was so much fun to play, and so fun to share, that it earned the first-ever VR platinum by selling over one million copies. More unique games like *Beat Saber* would tip the balance to sell more copies and, in turn, more headsets.

As for what the game will be, who knows? But the community will be watching for fun experiences to try out.

In the meantime, companies are exploring improved control methods; among other things, it is partially why

Facebook introduced hand tracking; few interactions are more seamless than using one's own hands. The company also announced that they are investigating brain interfaces, though it is unlikely to be released in 2020. Thom Strimbu, an Immersive Strategy Consultant, also notes that large companies will continue to consume smaller ones to develop their platforms.

Like with any prediction, it is extraordinarily challenging to point out when something is the 'year' of VR. Nor is it helpful. It shall arrive when it wants to come, and once it does, it will be when we do not expect it. VR in 2020 will still be fun, diverse, and exciting; enjoy surfing the wave.

One last thought. Sometimes, the smallest of immersive experiences can help and bring joy. It doesn't need to shake the world or change it; it can just leave a small yet powerful imprint on a small group. Jessica Driscoll found the same:

'Whilst shooting a 360 piece for Polio awareness for Rotary International in India we visited a hospital ward where our heroine the wonderful Alokita was in rehabilitation after several surgical procedures after contracting polio as a child. The surrounding wards were full of people who had been disabled by the disease and were far away from family and their homes. While setting up for the next shot we decided to show a 360 VR piece that Peter Collis shot for the Philharmonia orchestra in London, Mahler conducted by Esa Pekka Salonen. I don't think showing the piece had any medical impact on the patients and I am not claiming that but the pure pleasure of being transported to another world was evident during this impromptu session we had and an experience I will always treasure.'

We are living through an Immersive Reality Revolution, where major narrative threads will dictate how we, and several generations after us, will see this period of history. But for me, it's stories like these that I will remember.

ABOUT THE AUTHOR

T. P. Ffiske is the Editor of Virtual Perceptions, a website covering the latest trends in immersive reality. He graduated from the University of Exeter in 2015 and has worked in PR and communications since then. In that time, Tom has worked with Currys PC World, Oracle, PlayStation, BT, Western Digital, NTT, Avanade, Zappar, Virtual Umbrella, and Make Real.

He has a deep passion for immersive media, and he has reported and analysed the industry for over three years. In that time Tom has spoken at events, contributed his views to the BBC and the Times, and became a member of the BIMA Immersive Council.

In his spare time, he likes to write, read, and assist with the development of quidditch via Q Consultancy, a group of volunteers assisting players with the sport globally. He also has a cat called Bartimaeus and prefers to drink peppermint tea in the afternoon.

Website: www.virtualperceptions.com
Twitter: @TomFfiske

BIBLIOGRAPHY

"Apple Acquired Augmented Reality Headset Startup Vrvana for $30M." TechCrunch, http://social.techcrunch.com/2017/11/21/apple-acquires-mixed-reality-headset-startup-vrvana-for-30m/. Accessed 18 Feb. 2020.

"Apple Acquires Augmented Reality Company Metaio." TechCrunch, http://social.techcrunch.com/2015/05/28/apple-metaio/. Accessed 18 Feb. 2020.

"Apple Acquires Power Efficient LED Tech Company LuxVue." TechCrunch, http://social.techcrunch.com/2014/05/02/apple-acquires-power-efficient-led-tech-company-luxvue/. Accessed 18 Feb. 2020.

"Apple Acquires SMI Eye-Tracking Company." TechCrunch, http://social.techcrunch.com/2017/06/26/apple-acquires-smi-eye-tracking-company/. Accessed 18 Feb. 2020.

"Apple Patent Describes Tangibility Visualization of Virtual Objects within Various Headset Environments." Patently Apple, https://www.patentlyapple.com/patently-apple/2019/11/apple-patent-describes-tangibility-visualization-of-virtual-objects-within-various-headset-environments.html. Accessed 18 Feb. 2020.

"Audi Launches Virtual Reality Technology in Dealerships." Audi MediaCenter, https://www.audi-mediacenter.com:443/en/press-releases/audi-launches-virtual-reality-technology-in-dealerships-9270. Accessed 18 Feb. 2020.

"Beat Saber with Brie Larson" YouTube. https://www.youtube.com/watch?v=05pzUXujMJU. Accessed 18 Feb. 2020.

"Facebook Confirms It's Building Augmented Reality Glasses." TechCrunch, http://social.techcrunch.com/2018/10/24/facebook-ar-headset/. Accessed 18 Feb. 2020.

"Future of Storytelling : More immersive and interactive experiences Muki Kulhan GameChangers London" YouTube. https://www.youtube.com/watch?v=kIOa41Tm0Ko. Accessed 24 Feb. 2020.

"Global Eyewear Market Value 2018-2025." Statista, https://www.statista.com/statistics/300087/global-eyewear-market-value/. Accessed 18 Feb. 2020.

"How XR Environments Shape User Behavior." The Extended Mind, https://extendedmind.io/blog/2018/11/13/how-xr-environments-shape-user-behavior. Accessed 18 Feb. 2020.

"IAnimal - a Virtual Reality Experience into the Lives of Farmed Animals." IAnimal, https://ianimal.uk. Accessed 18 Feb. 2020.

"Masterworks: Journey Through History Provides A Transformative Educational VR Experience." VIVE Blog, 1 Oct. 2018, https://blog.vive.com/us/2018/10/01/masterworks_vr_experience/.

"Oculus Eclipses $100 Million in VR Content Sales." TechCrunch, http://social.techcrunch.com/2019/09/25/oculus-eclipses-100-million-in-vr-content-sales/. Accessed 18 Feb. 2020.

"Oculus Quest Devices Are Selling as Fast as Facebook Can Make Them." Android Central, 1 Aug. 2019, https://www.androidcentral.com/oculus-quest-selling-them-fast-we-can-make-them-according-zuckerberg.

"Rupert Breheny (Google): Enabling Immersive Exploration with Google Earth VR" YouTube. https://www.youtube.com/watch?v=sjqR90XGRDs. Accessed 24 Feb. 2020.

"SuperData: Oculus Quest Will Mainstream VR in 2019, but AR Will Lead by 2021." VentureBeat, 19 Oct. 2018, https://venturebeat.com/2018/10/19/superdata-oculus-quest-will-mainstream-vr-in-2019-but-ar-will-lead-by-2021/.

"VR Arcades Are Hot Trend, But Consumers Want So Much More." Greenlight Insights, 24 Feb. 2018, https://greenlightinsights.com/vr-arcades-consumers-want-more-location-based-vr/.

Bringing Augmented and Virtual Reality to the Classroom | Center for Information Technology and Society - UC Santa Barbara. https://cits.ucsb.edu/news/announcement/650. Accessed 18 Feb. 2020.

Can Augmented Reality Solve the Virtual Dressing Room Problem? – RetailWire. https://retailwire.com/discussion/can-augmented-reality-solve-the-virtual-dressing-room-problem/. Accessed 18 Feb. 2020.

Dolgin, Elie. "The Myopia Boom." Nature News, vol. 519, no. 7543, Mar. 2015, p. 276. www.nature.com, doi:10.1038/519276a.

Facts and Figures. https://www.actiononhearingloss.org.uk/about-us/our-research-and-evidence/facts-and-figures/. Accessed 24 Feb. 2020.

Ffiske, Tom, and Mandahus, Lena. "Virtually History: The Berlin Wall." Virtual Perceptions, 6 Nov. 2019, https://www.virtualperceptions.com/virtually-history-the-berlin-wall/.

Ffiske, Tom. "'Paint Me a Scene': How Is VR Storytelling Different?" Virtual Perceptions, 9 Nov. 2016, https://www.virtualperceptions.com/paint-me-a-scene-how-is-vr-storytelling-different/.

Ffiske, Tom. "Shifting Shopping Habits with VR." Virtual Perceptions, 24 Sept. 2018, https://www.virtualperceptions.com/shopping-habits-vr-infosys/.

Ffiske, Tom. "Virtual Reality in Education: What Is theFuture?" Virtual Perceptions, 22 Aug. 2019, https://www.virtualperceptions.com/virtual-reality-education-future/.

Ffiske, Tom. "Virtual Reality in the Retail Industry: How Will VR and AR Impact Shopping?" Virtual Perceptions, 22 Mar. 2019, https://www.virtualperceptions.com/virtual-reality-retail/.

Hamilton, Ian. "Sony Sold 4.2 Million PSVR Headsets." UploadVR, 25 Mar. 2019, https://uploadvr.com/sony-4-point-2-million-sold/.

Hayden, Scott. "'Beat Saber' Sells Over One Million Copies." Road to VR, 16 Mar. 2019, https://www.roadtovr.com/beat-saber-sells-one-million-copies/.

Hayden, Scott. "Facebook CEO: 'VR Is Taking Longer Than Expected, But We'll See It To Mass Adoption.'" Road to VR, 4 Nov. 2019, https://www.roadtovr.com/facebook-vr-longer-than-expected-mass-adoption/.

Hyken, Shep. "Starbucks Closes 8,000 Stores For Racial Bias Training -- Is It Enough?" Forbes, https://www.forbes.com/sites/shephyken/2018/06/01/starbucks-closes-8000-stores-for-racial-bias-training-is-it-enough/. Accessed 18 Feb. 2020.

Imagining a New Interface: Hands-Free Communication without Saying a Word. https://tech.fb.com/imagining-a-new-interface-hands-free-communication-without-saying-a-word/. Accessed 24 Feb. 2020.

Jensen, Lasse, and Flemming Konradsen. "A Review of the Use of Virtual Reality Head-Mounted Displays in Education and Training." Education and Information Technologies, vol. 23, no. 4, July 2018, pp. 1515–29. Springer Link, doi:10.1007/s10639-017-9676-0.

Kelly, Makena. "Microsoft Secures $480 Million HoloLens Contract from US Army." The Verge, 28 Nov. 2018, https://www.theverge.com/2018/11/28/18116939/microsoft-army-hololens-480-million-contract-magic-leap.

Lee, Dami. "How Ommy Akhe Makes Her Ultra-Cool Instagram AR Filters." The Verge, 22 Nov. 2019, https://www.theverge.com/2019/11/22/20963747/ommy-akhe-instagram-filters-spark-ar-augmented-reality.

McAloon, Alissa. 20% of the Oculus Store's $100 Million Lifetime Sales Were Quest Titles. /view/news/351136/20_of_the_Oculus_Stores_100_million_lifetime_sales_were_Quest_titles.php. Accessed 24 Feb. 2020.

McGuire, Laura Stone, and Ali Alaraj. "Competency Assessment in Virtual Reality-Based Simulation in Neurosurgical Training." Comprehensive Healthcare Simulation: Neurosurgery, edited by Ali Alaraj, Springer International Publishing, 2018, pp. 153–57. Springer Link, doi:10.1007/978-3-319-75583-0_12.

Nakamura, Lisa. "Virtual Reality and the Feeling of Virtue: Women of Color Narrators, Enforced Hospitality, and the Leveraging of Empathy." Proceedings of the 2019 on Designing Interactive Systems Conference - DIS '19, ACM Press, 2019, pp. 3–3. DOI.org (Crossref), doi:10.1145/3322276.3325420.

Parong, Jocelyn & Mayer, Richard. (2018). Learning Science in Immersive Virtual Reality. Journal of Educational Psychology. 10.1037/edu0000241.

PwC Seeing Is Believing Report. https://cloud.uk.info.pwc.com/seeing-is-believing-report-download. Accessed 18 Feb. 2020.

Ramirez, Erick Jose. "Ecological and Ethical Issues in Virtual Reality Research: A Call for Increased Scrutiny." Philosophical Psychology, vol. 32, no. 2, Feb. 2019, pp.

211–33. Taylor and Francis+NEJM, doi:10.1080/09515089.2018.1532073.

Regalado, Antonio. "Facebook Is Funding Brain Experiments to Create a Device That Reads Your Mind." MIT Technology Review, https://www.technologyreview.com/s/614034/facebook-is-funding-brain-experiments-to-create-a-device-that-reads-your-mind/. Accessed 24 Feb. 2020.

Reynolds, Matt. "How IKEA's Future-Living Lab Created an Augmented Reality Hit." Wired UK, Mar. 2018. www.wired.co.uk, https://www.wired.co.uk/article/ikea-place-augmented-reality-app-space-10.

Robertson, Adi. "Google Is Discontinuing the Daydream View VR Headset, and the Pixel 4 Won't Support Daydream." The Verge, 15 Oct. 2019, https://www.theverge.com/2019/10/15/20915609/google-pixel-4-no-daydream-support-view-vr-headset-discontinued.

Robertson, Adi. "Oculus Is Trying to Make the Quest the Only Home Headset That Matters." The Verge, 27 Sept. 2019, https://www.theverge.com/2019/9/27/20885082/oculus-quest-home-headset-lineup-oc6.

Sánchez Laws, Ana Luisa, and Tormod Utne. "Ethics Guidelines for Immersive Journalism." Frontiers in Robotics and AI, vol. 6, 2019. Frontiers, doi:10.3389/frobt.2019.00028.

Sankaranarayanan, Ganesh, et al. "Immersive Virtual Reality-Based Training Improves Response in a Simulated Operating Room Fire Scenario." Surgical Endoscopy, vol.

32, no. 8, Aug. 2018, pp. 3439–49. Springer Link, doi:10.1007/s00464-018-6063-x.

Sheikh, A., et al. Directing Attention in 360-Degree Video. Jan. 2016, pp. 29 (9 .)-29 (9 .). digital-library.theiet.org, doi:10.1049/ibc.2016.0029.

Slater, Mel, et al. "A Virtual Reprise of the Stanley Milgram Obedience Experiments." PLoS ONE, edited by Aldo Rustichini, vol. 1, no. 1, Dec. 2006, p. e39. DOI.org (Crossref), doi:10.1371/journal.pone.0000039.

Society, National Geographic. "Virtual Reality at Nat Geo." National Geographic Society, http://www.nationalgeographic.org/events/event/virtual-reality/. Accessed 18 Feb. 2020.

Statt, Nick. "Oculus Is Bringing Its Rift and Go VR Headsets to Classrooms around the World." The Verge, 28 Aug. 2018, https://www.theverge.com/2018/8/28/17792166/oculus-vr-rift-go-headsets-education-classrooms-taiwan-japan-seattle.

Sun, Leo. "Facebook's 3 Biggest Announcements From Oculus Connect 5." The Motley Fool, 30 Sept. 2018, https://www.fool.com/investing/2018/09/30/facebooks-3-biggest-announcements-from-oculus-conn.aspx.

Todd, Carolyn L. "Here's What Meditation Can—and Can't—Do for Your Health." SELF, https://www.self.com/story/mindfulness-meditation-health-benefits. Accessed 18 Feb. 2020.

Vuzix Expands Market Access for Vuzix Blade Smart Glasses to 35 Countries with the Addition of Japan :: Vuzix Corporation (VUZI). https://ir.vuzix.com/press-releases/detail/1676/vuzix-expands-market-access-for-vuzix-blade-smart-glasses. Accessed 18 Feb. 2020.

Weale, Sally, and Richard Adams. "'It's Dangerous': Full Chaos of Funding Cuts in England's Schools Revealed." The Guardian, 8 Mar. 2019. www.theguardian.com, https://www.theguardian.com/education/2019/mar/08/its-dangerous-full-chaos-of-funding-cuts-in-englands-schools-revealed.

Wright, Mike, and Ellie Zolfagharifard. "Internet Is Giving Us Shorter Attention Spans and Worse Memories, Major Study Suggests." The Telegraph, 6 June 2019. www.telegraph.co.uk, https://www.telegraph.co.uk/technology/2019/06/06/internet-giving-us-shorter-attention-spans-worse-memories-major/.

Young, Tyler. "This VR Founder Wants to Gamify Empathy to Reduce Racial Bias." Vice, 20 July 2018, https://www.vice.com/en_us/article/a3qeyk/this-vr-founder-wants-to-gamify-empathy-to-reduce-racial-bias.

Printed in Great Britain
by Amazon